SpringerBriefs in Philosophy

More information about this series at http://www.springer.com/series/10082

Minsoo Jung

An Investigation of the Causal Inference Between Epidemiology and Jurisprudence

 Springer

Minsoo Jung ⓘ
Dongduk Women's University
Seoul
Korea (Republic of)

ISSN 2211-4548   ISSN 2211-4556   (electronic)
SpringerBriefs in Philosophy
ISBN 978-981-10-7861-3   ISBN 978-981-10-7862-0   (eBook)
https://doi.org/10.1007/978-981-10-7862-0

Library of Congress Control Number: 2017963013

Printed on acid-free paper

This Springer imprint is published by the registered company Springer Nature Singapore Pte Ltd. part of
Springer Nature
The registered company address is: 152 Beach Road, #21-01/04 Gateway East, Singapore 189721, Singapore

Preface

By body I understand a mode that in a certain and determinate way expresses God's essence insofar as he is considered as an extended thing

Benedictus de Spinoza *Ethics*

The development of the natural sciences has gradually shed light on previously unknown causal relationships through scientific hypotheses and verifications. Given adequate time, the controversy over causal relationships between harmful materials and diseases will be mainly resolved. However, judges cannot wait and must determine legal value judgments on causal relationships as a requirement for the establishment of illegal acts. In other words, the responsibility to compensate for damages that have actually occurred must be imputed to a particular party. This book examined how legal causation inference and epidemiological causal inference can be harmonized within the realm of jurisprudence. It examined why legal causation and epidemiological causation differ from each other and the ensuing problems. This book also discussed how legal justice can be realized and how victims' rights can be protected. And it looked at the epidemiological evidence of causal relationships in cases such as smoking and the development of lung cancer. It also allowed readers to correctly interpret and rationally use the results of epidemiological studies in lawsuits. This book argued that in today's risk society, it is no longer possible to deny the competence of evidence from epidemiological research results. In particular, this book pointed out that the cases for which there is no way to prove causal relations except for epidemiological data will lead to an increase in lawsuits for damages as a result of harmful materials which affect our health. In other words, this book argued that the responsibility to compensate for damages that have actually occurred must be imputed to a particular party, and this can be done by understanding the causal inference between jurisprudence and epidemiology. This book serves as a foundation for students, academics, and researchers who have an interest in epidemiology and the law and are keen to find out how jurisprudence can bring them together.

I am deeply grateful to the many people who have provided helpful comments and encouragement. My appreciation is extended to U.-J. Pak and D.-K. Kim, Seoul National University School of Law; K. Viswanath, Harvard School of Public Health; and Chan S. Suh, Boise State University. This book came to fruition thanks in part to the stimulation and support of my family. Esther and Hoon have provided encouragement and love beyond measure. I also wish to express many thanks to my parents, whose patience and support sustained me while I wrote this book.

Seoul, Korea   Minsoo Jung
November 2017

Contents

1 Introduction 1
  1.1 Research Background 1
  1.2 Book Design 6
  References 7

2 Research Background 9
  2.1 Essential Review of Causation 10
  2.2 Causation in Philosophy 15
    2.2.1 Problem of Induction 15
    2.2.2 Causation in Empirical Philosophy 17
    2.2.3 Causation in the Philosophy of Law 23
  2.3 Causation in Criminal Law 27
    2.3.1 Theory of Objective Imputation and Criticisms ... 28
    2.3.2 Comparison with the Anglo-American Theory
           of Causation 29
    2.3.3 Application to the South Korean Criminal Act 30
    2.3.4 Legal Cases in Korea 31
    2.3.5 Remarks 33
  2.4 Causation in Civil Law 34
    2.4.1 Causation in Medical Malpractices 34
    2.4.2 Objects of Proof and the Burden of Proof 35
    2.4.3 Review of Judicial Precedents 36
    2.4.4 Remarks 39
  2.5 Causation in Epidemiology 40
  References 42

3 Methods in Epidemiology 45
  3.1 The Role of Epidemiology 45
  3.2 Epidemiological Investigation 46
    3.2.1 Experimental Study and Observational Study 46

      3.2.2   Types of Observational Study 47
  3.3 Interpretations of Epidemiological Results 48
      3.3.1   Relative Risk 48
      3.3.2   Odds Ratio 49
      3.3.3   Attributable Risk 50
  3.4 Causal Misinterpretations in Epidemiology 50
  References 53

4 Debates on Causation in Tobacco Lawsuits 55
  4.1 Legal Perspectives 56
  4.2 Epidemiological Perspectives 58
  4.3 Tobacco Lawsuit Cases in Korea 60
  References 66

5 Criteria of Epidemiological Causation and Its Limitations 69
  5.1 Criteria of Epidemiological Causation 69
  5.2 Critiques of the Epidemiological Criteria 72
  5.3 Pragmatic Pluralism in Causal Inference 72
      5.3.1   Potential Outcome Approach 73
      5.3.2   Restricted Potential Outcome Approach 75
      5.3.3   Difficult Points of RPOA 77
  5.4 Scientific Evidence in the Court 80
  5.5 Remarks 83
  References 84

6 Epidemiological Causation and Legal Causation 87
  6.1 Legal Proof on Causation with Epidemiological Results 87
  6.2 Legal Proof on Causation Without Epidemiological Results 90
  6.3 Remarks 91
  References 92

7 Conclusions 93
  7.1 Concluding Remarks 93
  7.2 Practical Implications 95
  References 99

Appendix 101

Index 107

Chapter 1
Introduction

Abstract Though it is based on scientific inferences and takes on a statistic and probabilistic nature, epidemiological evidence is often used at present in lawsuits in relation to damages. In particular, the point of contention in recent lawsuits for damages due to tobacco companies' illegal acts has been whether or not causal relations between smoking and diseases are proven by epidemiological data submitted by the plaintiffs as evidence. Although legal inferences based on correct causal relations are very important for realizing legal justice and for relieving victims, related research in terms of basic law has been insufficient. Consequently, the present study compares and analyzes legal causal inferences and epidemiological causal inferences to harmonize the two within the realm of jurisprudence.

1.1 Research Background

In April 2015, the National Health Insurance Service (NHIS) in South Korea brought lawsuits against Philip Morris International (PMI) Korea, British American Tobacco (BAT) Korea, and Korea Tomorrow & Global (KT & G; Korean Tobacco Firm). The NHIS thus raised tobacco lawsuits in South Korea, which possesses a national health insurance (NHI) system, because smoking causes various diseases, which in turn led to financial losses by the NHI due to the immense costs for treatment. Admittedly, the country had previously seen lawsuits raised by individuals with lung cancer or lung diseases against tobacco companies. However, because it was the first time for a state organization to bring lawsuits as a representative of the public interest, the cases received public attention. The main contents of these lawsuits were about a demand to the tobacco companies listed above for approximately 50 billion won that the NHIS had unnecessarily disbursed to 3500 patients with a smoking history of over 20 pack years and a smoking duration of over 30 years or cancer patients with specific carcinomas reported as likely to be caused by smoking (e.g., small-cell lung cancer, squamous cell lung cancer, and squamous cell laryngeal cancer). The present study reviews issues

M. Jung, *An Investigation of the Causal Inference Between Epidemiology and Jurisprudence*, SpringerBriefs in Philosophy, https://doi.org/10.1007/978-981-10-7862-0_1

including causality among tobacco companies' illegal acts, smoking, and lung cancer occurrence.

The key issue in a suit for damages resulted from illegal acts of tobacco firms is whether a causation between smoking and diseases can be proven, based on the epidemiological data submitted by the plaintiff as evidence. Proving the causation arises as the key issue in smoking-related lawsuits because the onset of lung cancer among smokers is affected by factors aside smoking and also because there is a long temporal gap between smoking and the onset of the disease. The usual damages which concern suits for damages can be explained by physical action such as bodily harm induced by fistfights, which has a short temporal gap between the cause and the effect (Jee, 2014: 1356–1369). In smoking-related lawsuits, however, smokers are exposed to tobacco smoke for decades and eventually contract the disease after the complex effects of other factors intervene. It is, therefore, difficult to determine the causation of how much each of the factors, including smoking, other unhealthy lifestyles, occupational risk or harmful environmental factors among others, has contributed to carcinogenesis.

Epidemiology is a study which focuses on how diseases are distributed among populations and on what determines such distribution (Gordis, 2013: 2–18). Epidemiological evidence is based on scientific inference and is statistical and stochastic but frequently used in suits for damages. For instance, the plaintiff who has the burden of proving the loss may argue that the plaintiff has contracted the disease Y because he/she was exposed to the risk factor X, on the grounds of an epidemiological study on the probability of a group exposed to the risk factor X to contract the disease Y. However, the defendant, the tobacco company, in this case, can refute this statement, arguing that the causation of the individual damage suffered by the plaintiff cannot be proven by the statistical and stochastic epidemiological evidence. Analysis and understanding on how the legal and scientific judgment on causation differs are necessary, but there is a lack of relevant research in the field of the philosophy of law.

Under Section 750 of the Civil Code, the requirement for the establishment of right of claim by illegal acts is as follows: (a) the intention or negligence by the defendant, (b) an illegal act, (c) damage of the plaintiff, and (d) causation between an illegal act and damage (Yang & Kwon, 2012). Here, the conventional opinion of the academia and judicial precedents adhere to the theory of proximate cause which disregards contingency and solely accepts causation based on high probability. That is, a proximate cause is established between two events when an event should commonly follow a preceding event.

Unlike in natural sciences, the burden of proof in legal causation is given to the person directly involved. The burden of proof is the disadvantage to legal judgment imposed on the parties to a suit in cases under which it is uncertain whether a fact that needs to be proved actually exists and, thus, is deemed nonexistent (Min & Kim, 2012). Under Section 202 of the Civil Proceedings Act, the court judges on the proof of a certain fact by freely evaluating the evidence, based on the principle of justice and equity, with the defense of the defendant and the examination of the evidence under account. The plaintiff has the burden of proof to claiming the liability for damages, and if he/she cannot prove that the defendant is responsible for the damages, the claim for liability for damages cannot legally be established.

Generally, the party with the burden of proof has a higher likelihood to lose a suit because it is difficult to legally prove the existence of causation. Thus, there has been effort to realize the plaintiff's relief of right in fields where the causation is difficult to prove.[1] For instance, for a suit on damages caused by air pollution, it is usual for the plaintiff to have been indirectly exposed to the contaminant produced by the defendant through the air or water for a long duration of time. The probability theory was devised to alleviate the burden of proof in such cases. According to the probability theory, proving the causation should not be likened to scientific verification and the probability of an event not happening if not for a harmful act would be sufficient (Jung & Yoo, 2014; Lee, 2015). The plaintiff shall sufficiently prove the considerable probability of a causation being established between the harmful act and the damage, and if the assailant cannot disproof this, he/she shall take the liability for damages.

Proof of causation by probability theory can be classified into two parts: the "factual presumption theory" through which the existence of causation can be presumed within the limits of free evaluation of evidence if a probable proof exists, and "the principle of superiority of evidence," according to which judicial relief is possible with the proof that one party's facts have a higher level of probability among the facts argued by the plaintiff and defendant (Min & Kim, 2012). The probability theory, however, received criticism for failing to realize the plaintiffs' relief, because if the degree of proof of the plaintiff can qualify as probability, the probability of the disproof presented by the defendant would also be sufficient (Jung & Yoo, 2014; Lee, 2015).

Thus, to strengthen the theoretical weak points of the probability, another argument, to alleviate the plaintiff's burden of proof by the doctrine of "res ipsa loquitur (the thing speaks itself)," was presented and now is currently adopted by the Supreme Court to alleviate the burden of proof (Jung & Yoo, 2014; Lee, 2015). In other words, if damages have occurred due to harmful materials produced by the assailant, the assailant cannot get away from the liability for damages unless he/she proves the harmlessness of the materials. In fact, in the Case 2000Da65666, the Supreme Court made decision that because it is difficult for the plaintiff to prove the causality of the damage caused by environmental pollution, the assailant shall be unable to get away from the liability for damages unless they prove that it is harmless. The Supreme Court also relaxed the burden of proof in the Case 2008Da17776, in which the plaintiffs who were suffering from hemophilia accused the defendant, the pharmaceutical company, of the unlawful act of negligence in production and supplying of blood products. The Court ruled that in cases concerning pharmaceuticals, which too can be classified as products, it would be ideal for the liability system to alleviate the burden of proof so that if there had been any

[1]The Decision of the Supreme Court of Korea 2000Da65666 (2002. 10. 22.); The Decision of the Supreme Court of Korea 2008Da17776 (2011. 9.29.)

defects in blood products produced by the pharmaceutical company and if the plaintiffs have been infected, the causation can be assumed and the liability for damages taken. The Court decided that in this case, the possibility of the plaintiff being infected by a virus can be used to infer causation, along with the use of the blood products, the temporal contiguity of infection, statistical associations, the manufacturing process of the blood products, and the medical characteristics of the infected virus.

However, the Supreme Court ruled differently in the tobacco case charged by smokers. In the 2011Da22092 Case, the plaintiffs, who smoked for a long time and contracted lung cancer, argued that the tobacco company was responsible for the disease by manufacturing cigarettes with defects in design and instruction in accordance to the product liability law. The Supreme Court, however, ruled that the original verdict, which denied the causation between smoking and the onset of non-small-cell lung cancer and bronchioalveolar carcinoma, is not unjust. The Supreme Court decided that such carcinoma are not specific diseases caused merely by smoking but are non-specific disease which can be contracted via complex effects between the external and environmental factors and intrinsic factors. In conclusion, the Supreme Court deemed that the epidemiological evidence presented by the plaintiffs were insufficient to prove the probability of the lung cancer to be caused by smoking. Moreover, the Supreme Court dismissed the appeal on the grounds that there are no defects in the manufacturing and design of the cigarettes produced by the defendants.

In fact, the Supreme Court has been applying the legal principle of distinguishing specific disease from non-specific disease, ever since the suit for damages brought by the Vietnam War veterans against defoliant manufacturers. Specific diseases, according to the Supreme Court Classification, are diseases which are induced by a single cause and the cause (the specific cause of a disease) of which directly corresponds to the result (the onset of a disease). The concept of specific diseases, however, is controversial because it is not a concept commonly used in the health and medical care field (Porta et al., 2014; Rothman, Greenland, & Lash, 2008: 5–31). The concept of specific diseases came into being because chloracne was classified as a specific disease due to the misreading of a report from the U.S. National Academy of Science in the original trial.[2] The original trial ruled that since chloracnes are only found among people who were exposed to TCDD, it can serve as a biomarker which distinguishes one's exposure to TCDD. Specificity is an indicator which can quite accurately predict the occurrence of a factor when another factor exists among two correlated factors (Rothman et al., 2008: 51–70). In reality, however, it is mostly meaningless to determine a specific relation in the onset of diseases.

Epidemiologists have reservations on having specificity as a criterion for proving epidemiological associations and causation (Gordis, 2013: 243–261; Rothman & Greenland, 2005). For example, the causation between X and Y should not be

---

[2]The Decision of the Appellate Court of Seoul 2002Na32662 (2006. 1. 26.)

easily rejected because the possibility of the factor X to cause the disease Y is low. It is hard to say that the relation between lung cancer and smoking is specific, because lung cancer can occur from various causes aside smoking and due to the fact that smoking can cause various diseases aside lung cancer. Causality, however, can be assumed because smokers have a 10 times higher relative risk of developing lung cancer than non-smokers (US Surgeon General's Advisory Committee on Smoking and Health, 1964). In the end, it is dangerous to conclude that there is no causation on the grounds that there are no or little specificity in the causal reasoning process based on epidemiological relativity (Hill, 1965).

A great number of epidemiologists are questioning whether it is necessary to apply the concept of specific diseases in the process of judging the reliability of epidemiological evidence (Lee, 2016). It is, therefore, reasonable to verify the causation between the risk factor and the disease by considering all diseases as non-specific diseases and to put the intensity of epidemiological relativity into consideration. Moreover, the Supreme Court requires the plaintiff to prove not only the epidemiological relativity but also the individual circumstances for the liability for damages of the defendant to be established in a ruling cases raised by smokers against cigarette firms. In this situation, however, the plaintiff's, that is, the victim's, relief of right is too severely restricted.

When the epidemiological evidence shows such a strong relevance between risk factors within populations and the onset of diseases that the possibility of developing the disease by individual contingency is virtually nonexistent, it would be reasonable to have the defendant prove that the disease was not caused by the specific risk factor but from other factors, rather than having the plaintiff prove that their individual situations have not affected the onset of the disease. To have plaintiffs prove that "other factors" are irrelevant to their diseases is to have them practice the so-called proving of nonexistence.

Epidemiology should not be dismissed for being unable to provide valuable information on individuals, just because it conducts research with populations as its subject and because it draws conclusion on the probability at the population level by using parameters such as relative risk and attributable risk. For instance, the probability of causation calculated in epidemiology refers to the probability of the patient who was randomly selected from a group to have developed a disease due to a risk factor (Rothman et al., 2008: 5–31), which is extremely useful in converting the group-level probability to the individual-level. Accordingly, if the probability of causation can be assumed due to high epidemiological relevance, it would be just for the plaintiff to take the responsibility for refuting the presumed causation by proving other individual circumstances (Yune, 2011). If multiple factors should contribute to the onset of the disease, it would be appropriate to conclude that causation can be established between each factor and the onset of the disease[3], but to apply the legal principle of comparative negligence by calculating exactly how much each factor contributed to the development of the disease when determining

---

[3]The Decision of the Supreme Court of Korea 99Da43448·99Da43455 (2000. 1. 14.)

the range of the liability of damages (Section 763 and 396 of the Civil Code). In conclusion, it is important to acknowledge the difference between the scientific and legal causal inference, but to find a balance between them, so there would be no injustice for the victims' relief of right. It is especially important to examine the significance and usage of epidemiological data on proving legal in the field of the philosophy of law.

1.2 Book Design

While smoking has been known to be a cause of the development of lung cancer through diverse studies over the past several decades, the position of the South Korean Supreme Court in lawsuits for damages filed by individual smokers against tobacco companies has been that the development of lung cancer is an individual responsibility. In addition, the countless pieces of epidemiological evidence of the causal relationship between smoking and the development of lung cancer submitted to law courts have not been acknowledged as proof for legal judgments. Consequently, the present study examines how and why legal causation and epidemiological causation differ from each other and what the ensuing problems are. The structure of the present study is as follows. First, Chapter 1 describes the background and necessity of the research through tobacco lawsuits that are currently under way in South Korea. Next, Chap. 2 examines the differences and main characteristics of the determination of causal relationships per academic discipline. Starting with the roots of the concept of causal relationships, it analyzes the problem of causality in empirical philosophy and addresses the characteristics and major concepts of the determination of causal relationships in both criminal law and civil law. In addition, this chapter examines the determination of epidemiological causation between risk causes and the development of diseases mainly used in claims for damages today. Chapter 3 addresses epidemiological methodologies in order to examine carefully causal inferences in epidemiology. In particular, it examines how causation between events is established in epidemiology through experiments or observations as well as concepts used in the inference of causation such as that of relative risk and the possibility of biases in interpretations. Chapter 4 classifies the problem of determining causality in tobacco lawsuits into the legal perspective and the epidemiological perspective and compares the two and addresses major judicial precedents. Chapter 5 examines the criteria and limitations of determining epidemiological causation. In particular, it presents the perspective of pragmatic pluralism as a way for harmoniously using epidemiological proof in jurisprudence. Next, Chap. 6 compares judicial precedents that acknowledged epidemiological proof in determining legal causation and those that did not. Finally, based on foregoing discussions, Chap. 7 discusses how the two are to be harmonized in jurisprudence in order to realize legal justice along with the protection of victims' rights.

References

Gordis, L. (2013). *Epidemiology* (5th ed.). London, UK: Saunders.

Hill, A. B. (1965). The environment and disease: association or causation? *Proceedings of the Royal Society of Medicine, 58*(5), 295–300.

Jee, W. L. (2014). *Lecture on civil law* (12th ed.). Seoul: Hongmoonsa. (In Korean).

Jung, D. Y., & Yoo, B. H. (2014). *Civil procedure law*. Seoul: Pakyoungsa. (In Korean).

Lee, S. Y. (2015). *New civil procedure law* (10th ed.). Seoul, Korea: Pakyoungsa. (In Korean).

Lee, S. G. (2016). Proving causation with epidemiological evidence in tobacco lawsuits. *Journal of Preventive Medicine and Public Health, 49,* 80–96.

Min, I. Y., & Kim, N. H. (2012). *Annotated civil procedure law 1*. Seoul: Korean Association for Public Administration and Justice. (in Korean).

Porta, M. S., Greenland, S., Hernán, M., Santos Silva, I. D., Last, J. M., & International Epidemiological Association. (2014). *A dictionary of epidemiology*. (6th ed.). Oxford, UK: Oxford University Press.

Rothman, K. J., & Greenland, S. (2005). Causation and causal inference in epidemiology. *American Journal of Public Health, 95*(Suppl. 1), S144–S150.

Rothman, K. J., Greenland, S., & Lash, T. L. (Eds.). (2008). *Modern Epidemiology* (3rd ed.). New York, NY: Lippincott Williams & Wilkins.

US Surgeon General's Advisory Committee on Smoking and Health. (1964). *Smoking and health; report of the advisory committee to the Surgeon General of the Public Health Service.* Washington, DC: US Department of Health, Education, and Welfare, Public Health Service.

Yang, C. S., & Kwon, Y. J. (2012). *Changes and protection of rights: civil law 2*. Seoul: Pakyoungsa. (In Korean).

Yune, J. S. (2011). The main issues of the product liability. *Yonsei Law Review, 21*(3), 1–55. (In Korean).

Chapter 2
Research Background

Abstract Theories and judicial precedents follow the theory of proximate causal relations, which only acknowledges causal relations based on a high degree of probability while excluding contingencies. However, unlike the natural sciences, legal causal inferences impose the burden of proof on one party. Consequently, in cases where causal relations are difficult to prove, such as air pollution lawsuits, the theory of probability, which mitigates the plaintiffs' burden of proof, is used. According to this, to prove a causal relationship, strictness of the natural sciences is not required, and a substantial degree of probability that the results would not have occurred without the harmful acts in question alone is sufficient. This has developed into the legal principle that the plaintiffs' burden of proof is mitigated according to the prima facie rule and that when damages have been caused by harmful materials generated by the offenders, the responsibility to compensate the victims for damages cannot be avoided unless the harmlessness of the materials can be proven. According to the South Korean Civil Procedure Act, court judges whether or not a particular fact has been proven in consideration of the tenor of oral proceedings and the results of examinations of evidence and through free evaluations of evidence based on the ideas of justice and equity. However, although the protection of the rights of the victims has been strengthened in claims for compensation for damages due to harmful factors since the legislation of South Korea's Product Liability Act, the fact that long-term smoking leads to the development of lung cancer has not been acknowledged in smoking-related lawsuits. The emergence of modern philosophy and the development of the empirical sciences led to full-fledged discussions of causality. In particular, David Hume defined cause as proximity in space, priority in time, and necessary connections from an empirical perspective. In other words, he argued that an object could be called a cause when it preceded and was proximate to another object and always yielded a particular reaction under a particular condition. In addition, Hume saw causal pathways between agents' actions and the results as inductively inferred and the law of cause and effect as acquiring validity owing to its function of explaining events. These were termed inferences to the best explanation. Here, Hume saw cognitive subjects' creation of inevitable impressions under the particular condition mentioned above as the fundamental nature of causal relations as judged by human understanding, thus creating a point

M. Jung, *An Investigation of the Causal Inference Between Epidemiology and Jurisprudence*, SpringerBriefs in Philosophy, https://doi.org/10.1007/978-981-10-7862-0_2

of connection between objective judgments from facts and normative judgments. Although judgments in accordance with empirical rules are based on factual relations, judgments of the purposiveness of human actions must be addressed in relation to normative causal relations. For example, judging whether a criminal defendant's intended action led to predictable results or if a rupture arises in causal relations due to elements such as the action of a third party can be a question in criminal policy. These types of questions form the reason behind the support of what is termed the theory of objective imputation, according to which no act is to be punished for its results when it is not connected to the occurrence of danger, which is an element of crime, in terms of criminal law. This helps to determine the matter of the responsibility of agents in criminal law, which requires normative value judgments through the concept of substantiality or the possibility of foreknowledge. When the criteria for imputation are abstract and normative, dangers cannot be determined easily, and when crimes of omission are considered, it is difficult logically to connect the imputation of responsibility. On the other hand, civil law addresses the responsibility for default or for illegal acts based on factual causation. Consequently, only factual causation through which claims for compensation for damages can be acknowledged based on the theory of proximate causal relations is determined. However, in medical malpractice lawsuits, it is difficult for patients, who are the plaintiffs, to prove the existence of a causal relationship between their medical providers' medical practices and damages in such a way that judges will be convinced of a high degree of probability. Consequently, in cases such as those where violent presumptions are possible, statistical possibility is high, or causes other than the one in question could not have intervened, the plaintiffs' burden of proof is mitigated.

2.1 Essential Review of Causation

Immanuel Kant argued for the universal validity of the causal principle, and David Hume claimed that causation must be seen from an empirical perspective. Because such theories of causation still wield influence even now, the present study reviews both existing discussions and theories of causation that are discussed in the social sciences including jurisprudence today. Because its objects are human acts that it regulates, criminal law ponders on ways to determine causes and effects whose objects are humans instead of physical environments or which address human acts. The present study reviews event models and agent models of causation.

Kant saw all objective changes as occurring as a result of the association between cause and effect, calling this *the universal validity of the causal principle* (Watkins, 2005). According to the quantum theory today, however, the causal principle that occurs in the sphere of minute particles equal to or smaller than atoms can be described only through the law of probability. According to Werner Heisenberg's uncertainty principle, the awareness of event E1 is only probable with respect to the occurrence of E2, another event (Hoeffe & Ameriks, 2009). Hume defined cause as proximity, priority, and necessary connections from an empirical perspective. In other words, an object can be called a cause when it precedes and is proximate to another object and always yields particular reactions under particular conditions (Robison, 1977). Hume argued that cause and effect were only connected by proximity, priority, and necessary connections and not sustained by any other tie and that the conventional relationship between cause and effect was problematic (Strawson, 2014). Isaac Newton's classical physics saw time and space as absolute (natural constants) and velocity as subjective and relative (natural variable). However, the absoluteness of time and space is denied and the two are relativized by Albert Einstein's theory of relativity (Strawson, 2014). Because theories of causation in criminal law, whose objects are human acts, confirm issues that have been reconstructed in law courts in accordance with experience rules, discussions ensuing from scientific accomplishments such as those above do not pose a problem. However, *possible explanations of events* explicated by Kant and *proximity* and *conventional relationships* claimed by Hume can be important standards even for discussions on causation in criminal law today.

Theories of causation are discussed in all fields including the natural sciences and the social sciences. Because criminal jurisprudence, too, is a branch of the social sciences, it is necessary to examine theories of causation that are discussed in the social sciences today. Research in the social sciences, which adopt the position of the empirical sciences, sees the regularity of the causal order that emerges in social phenomena not as deterministic but as plastic (Imbens & Rubin, 2015: 3–21). Such plasticity can be examined in terms of four aspects.

First, the causal pathways through which a particular social phenomenon is generated are inferred inductively. In other words, regularity is detected by tracking cases that share particular types of causal pathways and generalizing these types. Second, neither can all causes leading to a social phenomenon be tracked without exception nor can a social phenomenon be said to result from a single cause. Third, there exists an unbridgeable, inherent gap between the world of causal inference and the actual world. Nor does the inference of causation according to logical scales confirm the existence of causation. In addition, even when causes resulting in a particular phenomenon have been derived logically, the inevitable causal mechanisms that lead such causes to bring about particular results cannot be determined. Fourth, because humans' orientation of action, orientation of value, and orientation of mentality are by no means eternal, social phenomena resulting from human interactions likewise are variable, and causation among social phenomena therefore is fluid.

In such a context, most studies in the empirical sciences accept the causation derived as a *probable relationship* that is effected when conditions precedent have been satisfied. Nor is causation in criminal law much different from causation discussed in the social sciences. In other words, causal pathways between an agent's acts and the results are inferred inductively, the agent's causes are seen not as *necessary and sufficient conditions* but as *sufficient conditions* or *necessary conditions*, the inherent gap between the world of causal inference and the actual world is acknowledged, and the relationship between cause and effect is viewed as a *probable relationship.* We thus need to examine the attributes of the principle of cause and effect.

According to traditional metaphysicians, one event became the cause of another because of particular, special *force*, and one event (cause) led to another (effect) because of such force (Loux, 2006: 17–20). Hume explained A bringing about B as A preceding B temporally, A touching B spatially, and anything similar to A always being followed by anything similar to B. The link connecting such ideas was causation, and the principle of cause and effect based on the natural properties of objects was explicated through the attributes of relationships among phenomena (Loux, 2006: 21–39). The purpose of science lies in obtaining knowledge based on the experienced world and generalizing and establishing that knowledge as experience rules. When causation has been determined according to such experience rules, individual causation constitutes the realization of a single law as an example. The principle of cause and effect acquires its validity through such *explanatory functions* (Heathcote & Armstrong, 1991: 63–74).

Although physics argues that objects are dominated solely by causation, organisms determine (i.e., *selbstgestaltung*) and regulate (i.e., *selbstregulation*) themselves at the stage of manifestation (Koons, 2000: 1–14). Correlation signifies a systematic interrelation between one factor and another. When human acts intervene, however, a correlation between factors A and B does not directly or immediately signify that either A or B is the other's cause. It is therefore necessary to understand the concept of categories in understanding causation in human acts. Categories increase the efficiency of communication and make predictions possible (Koons, 2000: 19–30). Consequently, in judging causation in accordance with human acts, purposiveness, correlations, and categorical judgments must be taken into consideration, unlike in the case of physical systems. With the goal orientation of human acts as a premise, it must be possible to explain how causation regulates human acts. Unlike causation in physical systems, this includes substantial and proximate causation. It is the so-called proximate causal relation. As a result, causation in human acts and causation in the physical sphere are distinguished by *agent models* and *event models*, respectively (Loux, 2006: 46–81; Koons, 2000: 77–90). While event models determine external aspects and role relationships, agent models determine internal motives. While causing events have no ontological responsibility for caused events according to event models, there is real responsibility between the two according to agent models.

The contents examined hitherto have the following implications for discussions on causation in criminal law. First, causation in criminal law must be examined after classification into factual relations and normative relations. Judgments according to experience rules must be based on factual relations, and judgments regarding purposiveness in human acts must be addressed in terms of normative causation, respectively. Second, laws that explain causation must be comprehensible and predictable to agents. Members of the public must be able to understand which acts constitute crimes, and explanations of such acts must include categorical judgments. Only then can judges presiding over lawsuits use such categories as scales for judgments. Third, while judgments regarding factual relations follow "but-for" causation (i.e., *sine qua non*), causation judgments regarding normative relations must determine whether or not a cause is *substantial* and *proximate* in leading to an effect.

In jurisprudence, German theories of causation have been mainly reviewed, and Anglo-British theories of causation have attracted little interest. In particular, British law courts have seen causation as an issue belonging to common sense and therefore not requiring philosophical analyses and only concerning the judgment of facts by the jury (Worrall & Moore, 2012). Theories of causation in the UK and the USA largely distinguish between factual causation and legal causation (Worrall & Moore, 2012).

Also called "but-for" causation, factual causation is of the position that when there is a relationship where the results would not have occurred without the defendants' acts, "but-for" causation exists between the defendants' acts and the results (Herring, 2010: 89–105). In fact, causation is so comprehensive that, in most cases, specific legal causes are assumed. In other words, legal causation determines normative causation after positivistic reviews in accordance with "but for." Here, normative judgments are made and criminal justice policy is taken into consideration (Keyserlink, 1994). In law, *causes* refer to operating and substantial causes. Here, *substantial causes* are causes that are not minor and are serious with respect to the results. In addition, the defendants' acts must have *caused* the causes of the results (Battaglini, 1952).

At times, there arise the phenomena of disconnections in causation. These refer, for example, to third parties' acts, acts of victims, and natural disasters. In case there exist third parties' free and arbitrary interventions, which the defendants cannot change, between the first acts and the results, causation is disconnected. In other words, third parties' free, voluntary, and informed acts lead to disconnections in causation, and causation is not completed even when causes that are substantial enough to give rise to the results have not been satisfied (Keyserlink, 1994: 92–95). In a case where the defendant stabbed the victim so that the latter was taken to the hospital but the victim, who had diatheses, died due to the physician's misadministration of drugs, the court ruled that the physician was not responsible for the victim's death because the former had little likelihood of foreseeing the latter's diatheses (Keyserlink, 1994: 96). Law courts determine whether an act constitutes the victim's act disconnecting causation with foreseeability (i.e., foreknowledge possibility) as the standard. When the defendant has performed an intended act and the foreseen results have occurred, this is called the intended results doctrine. In a case where the defendant gave the nurse poison to kill a baby but the latter hid it and a five-year-old gave that poison to another child and led the latter to die, the court acknowledged the defendant's murder (Keyserlink, 1994: 105). Having inherited British common law, the USA differs little from the UK in theories of causation. The defendants' acts must be the causes of the actual results, and "but-for" causation, according to which the results would not have occurred without the defendants' acts, must be effected. On the other hand, even when such factual causation has been acknowledged, legal responsibilities are imposed only when the requirement that the defendants have legal responsibilities for the caused results has been satisfied (LaFave, 2010: 2–76).

Factual causation: In American law, factual causation consists of determining, regardless of criminal liability for the results that have occurred, whether there is actual causation between the defendants' acts and the prohibited results. Here, "but for" (i.e., *sine qua non*) is used. In other words, if the answer to the question "Would the results have occurred without the defendants' acts?" is "No," then the defendants are judged to be responsible (Worrall & Moore, 2012). As has been examined above, factual causation reviews the British common law tradition and "but-for" causation in the Model Penal Code (MPC; Moore, 2009). Although the best review method according to this theory of conditions is counterfactual tests, reviewing necessity and sufficiency is a strong alternative due to problems (Spellman & Kincannon, 2001).

Proximate causation: Legal causation originates from the legal maxim that proximate causes rather than remote causes are important (Kelley, 1991). So-called proximate causality acknowledges causation regarding results either intended by the defendants or brought about by their acts. In other words, necessary is the requirement that a risk relationship proximate to the results that have occurred was either intended or hazarded (LaFave, 2010: 2–76). After factual causation is reviewed according to "but-for" causation, proximate causality is reviewed. Here, the jury excludes the defendants' acts that lack substantiality in accordance with common sense (Black, 2000). Legal causation applies to both intentional crimes and criminal negligence, and its judgment standards are substantiality, dangerousness, and a possibility of expectation to legal acts, as has been examined above. In the end, legal causation is an issue of who is criminally liable for crime.

Legal causation determines in actual issues whether or not the defendants' acts have led to the results via natural and probable consequences. Here, important are judgments regarding whether interventions disconnecting causation existed. Such intervening elements must occur after the defendants' acts, must have been unforeseeable at the time of the defendants' acts, must be the sole major cause of the results, and must be independent of the defendants' acts (Dix, 2009: 7–19). Although the interpretation of judicial precedents differs for each scholar, the standards of foreseeability and the substantiality of intervening causes are applied commonly.

When examined with foreseeability as the standard, intervening causes can be classified into *independent intervening causes* and *dependent intervening causes*. Independent intervening causes refer to cases that the defendants could have neither intended nor reasonably foreseen, and causation is disconnected here. Dependent intervening causes refer to cases that the defendants intended or were reasonably able to foresee. For example, in a case where a robber got in a car and demanded the victim to hand over the vehicle with a gun, and the victim stepped on the accelerator to escape but was hit by a bus and died, the car robber is responsible for the death. It is because, in this case, intervening causes are dependent on the results (Worrall & Moore, 2012).

In terms of the substantiality of intervening causes, when intervening causes have a more serious effect than do the causes created by the defendants, the defendants' criminal liability can constitute circumstances precluding wrongfulness. For example, when Brian has shot Michael with a 22 caliber handgun and Carl has shot with a 50 caliber rifle at the same time, Carl will be responsible for murder because he has provided a proximate cause of the death and Bill will be indicted for attempted murder (Worrall & Moore, 2012: 121). When there are voluntary victim interventions, however, the defendants are not criminally liable for the results.

As has been hitherto examined, Anglo-American law classifies causation into factual causation and legal causation and determines legal causation with the standards of substantiality and foreseeability. In particular, in the USA, either factual causation is reviewed or proximate causality is taken into consideration according to the theory of conditions (Moore, 2009: 84). According to proximate causality, causation is denied when cause and effect are too remote from each other or other independent causes exist (Robinson, 2008). In the USA, the judgment standards for proximate causality are substantiality, dangerousness, foreseeability, and substantiality of intervening causes.

2.2   Causation in Philosophy

2.2.1   Problem of Induction

The most systematic effort to learn from experience called empirical science is dubbed problem of induction by David Hume in the eighteenth century (Hume, 1975: 25–39). He asked why past experience was considered a guide to future experience (for him, this encompassed a complex problem in terms of the philosophy of mind). For example, one expects the sun to rise from the east tomorrow, too, because it has always done so throughout one's life. In Hume's view, such presumption does not originate from transcendental deduction which does not require experience (Hume, 1975: 60–79). For diverse beliefs obtained from experience, their opposites can be imagined. In other words, it is possible to imagine that the sun will not be able to rise tomorrow. This differs from transcendental statements where logical antinomies are impossible. One's knowledge of future experience can be derived only from experience, not from transcendental deductions. Successful learning knowledge is obtained from past experience. If the sun has been observed to rise from the east for a prolonged period, the same will hold true in the future as well. However, there is no basis whatsoever for the belief that future experience will be similar to past experience. Such a form of inductive justification is considered premise circularity where the conclusion of premise demonstration constitutes a part of that premise. This is because the conclusion to be proven has already been hypothesized as being true.

Induction refers to all inferences considered to be operations aimed at minimally true results that must be seen as constituting a type of inference, although such results are not deductively valid (Lipton, 2004). The problem is that inductive inferences in reality are far more complex than those based on repetitive events cited by Hume as examples. Such examples can be found in natural sciences where the advancement of knowledge is systematically performed. In science, the conclusion of an inference differs completely from the ground used for that inference in most cases. Upon observation, the spectrum of electromagnetic radiation emitted from a star far removed from the Earth tends toward color red. Redshifts are even more pronounced in the spectra of more distant stars. From this, scientists infer that starts are growing distant from the Earth, with those further removed growing distant at an even faster rate. This inference is not based on the past experience that redshifts have been observed in the spectra of stars hitherto seen. Instead, such explanations are based on the theory of unbiased emission patterns of electromagnetic radiation determined by Doppler effects and structural components. Although considerably different from examples examined above, consequent explanations are also inductive inferences.

Hypotheses regarding redshifts can be disproven by new observations as well. However, until disproven, they are accepted by scientific circles in the name of the so-called inference to the best explanation. A scientist will explain the reason for the sun's unfailing rise from the east as the rotation of the Earth, not as the fact that it has been observed by many people. This implies that many reflective inductive inferences are not simple extrapolations from existing proof. Instead, they encompass multi-stage inferential processes based on theory, although non-reflective behavior is based on the expectation that future experience will be similar to past experience in many cases. Such inferences to the best explanation are very similar to epidemiological explanations.

While empirical sciences are systematic and reflective efforts to learn from past experiences, it is unclear how rational inferences can be derived from experiences. Nevertheless, one learns through experiences. Consequently, it will be more accurate to say that one does not fully know how things learned from past experiences are to be justified. The question of how inferences can be justified serves as a ground for judgment in natural sciences and court decisions alike. Consequently, the problem of induction is an essential one where inferences are justified based on diverse facts. When many scientists ponder on study designs, evaluate how much data support hypotheses, and seek to elucidate what experimental manipulations or interventions will lead to expected results, one comes to face this problem of justifying inductive inference.

Hume's philosophical crux concerned how the conclusion of an inductive inference was related to its premise. A tool to derive a deductively valid conclusion from a premise is logical necessity. Inductive inferences also have a similar tool called causation. For Hume, a causal relationship was an adhesive connecting the premise and the conclusion of an inductive inference (Hume, 1975: 60–79). Although causal inferences themselves cannot justify inductions, causal knowledge is a very useful detour for explaining relationships among events. For example, the reason for the sun's rise from the east can be explained as follows. The movement of an astronomical object around its own fixed axis is called a rotation. Because the Earth rotates from the west to the east, the sun makes a diurnal motion from the east to the west. Consequently, one observes the sun rise from the east every day. In other words, because the Earth makes a counterclockwise movement from the west to the east, the sun, which is actually still, in contrast seems to move from the east to the west. This is the same principle as the phenomenon that when one looks outside from a moving vehicle, trees by the road seem to recede.

A detour through causation can better explain the inductive praxis in which one realistically engages. If one can state what causation and causal knowledge are, one can also state how good inductive inferences can be made through them. In addition, good and bad inferences can be distinguished by using causal inferences in the correct way.

2.2.2 Causation in Empirical Philosophy

The emergence of modern philosophy and the development of empirical sciences have led to full-fledged discussions of causality. According to Hume, the notion of cause and effect is a complex idea that consists of three foundational ideas: priority in time, proximity in space, and a necessary connection. Concerning priority in time, if I say that event A causes event B, one implication is that A occurs prior to B. If B were to occur before A, it would be absurd to say that A was the cause of B. Concerning the idea of proximity, if I say that A causes B, I mean B is in proximity to, or close to, A. For example, if I throw a rock and a window in China breaks at that moment, I would not conclude that my rock broke that window on the other side of the world. The broken window and the rock must be in close proximity to each other. However, priority and proximity alone do not constitute our entire notion of causality. For example, if I sneeze and lights go out, I would not conclude that my sneeze was the cause, despite the fact that conditions of priority and proximity were both fulfilled. We also believe that there is a necessary connection between cause A and effect B. During the modern period of philosophy, philosophers believe that a necessary connection is a power or force that connects two events. When billiard ball A strikes billiard ball B, there is a power that one event imparts the other. In keeping with his empiricist copy thesis that all ideas were copied from impressions, Hume tried to uncover the experience that gave rise to our notions of priority, proximity, and necessary connection. The first two are easy to explain. Priority traces back to our various experiences of time, while proximity traces back to our various experiences of space. However, what is the experience that gives us the idea of necessary connection? This notion of necessary connection is the specific focus of Hume's analysis of cause and effect.

Hume's view is that our proper idea of necessary connection is like a secondary quality formed by the mind. It is not a feature of the external world like a primary quality. First, he skeptically argues that we cannot gain an idea of necessary connection by observing it through our sensory experiences (Hume, 1978: 1.3.14.12). We have no external sensory impression of causal power when we observe cause and effect relationships. All that we ever see is cause A constantly conjoined with effect B. It does not arise from an internal impression such as when we introspectively reflect on willed bodily motions or when we will the creation of thoughts. These internal experiences are too elusive. Nothing in them can give content to our idea of necessary connection. Second, the idea that we have for necessary connection arises as follows. We experience a constant conjunction of events A and B (repeated sensory experiences where events resembling A are always followed by events resembling B). This produces a habit such that upon any further appearance of A, we expect B to follow. This in turn produces an internal feeling of expectation "to pass from an object to the idea of its usual attendant." It is from such impression that the idea of necessary connection is copied (Hume, 1978: 1.3.14.20). Third, a common but mistaken notion regarding this topic is that necessity resides within objects themselves. He explains this mistaken belief in terms of natural tendency we have to impute subjectively perceived qualities to external things (Hume, 1978: 1.3.14.24).

When someone makes a hit at a billiard ball with another, balls' movements are generally predicted in consideration of aspects including the speed of the moving ball, the angle at which balls collide with each other, and the condition of the floor on which one of the balls rolls. In addition, such predictions and results usually do not exceed the scope of common sense notwithstanding differences in the degree. For example, it is difficult for the ball that is struck to soar into the sky suddenly or to move in the direction opposite of the collision. Nevertheless, such cases can be imagined because they are not logical contradictions. If so, then why specific causes always are used to predict specific results followed? Hume found a problem with causation in humans' tendency to prefer specific results despite the possibility of predicting a countless number of cases through imagination. This tendency neither constitutes a priori reasoning nor indicates that results are already inherent in causes. According to Hume, such a tendency is shaped by habits formed which are affected by existing similar examples or cases.

Hume has defined cause in causation in two ways (Hume, 1978). First, cause temporally precedes and is spatially proximate to another object. All objects that are similar to the former are spatially proximate to objects that are similar to the latter (C1). Next, cause temporally precedes, is spatially proximate to, and has an association with another object. Here, ideas about one object form ideas about another, while impressions of one object prompt the mind to form vivid ideas about another (C2). The first definition only describes the objective state because objects' temporal and spatial arrangements are already open. The second definition is somewhat subjective because it uses terms such as "mind" not appearing earlier, "ideas," and "impressions" which are types of perceptions. At a glance, these two definitions might seem to be describing the single concept of cause in opposite ways. Grasping Hume's reasons for defining one concept in two opposite ways is important to philosophically determine causation.

Robinson has proposed that Hume had two goals. On the level of philosophical analysis, the first consists of the task of analyzing and clarifying the concept of cause (C1) (Robinson, 1962). On a psychological level, the second is to present an empirical law through definitions of cause (C2). Here, C1 and C2 are not equivalents because they are unequal denotatively or connotatively. Elements of sets corresponding to each definition do not match one another either. The definitions differ from one another as well.

First, when elements constituting the first definition are established as ordered pairs (x, y) of the occurrence of individual events and sets of these ordered pairs are established as C1 (x, y), respectively, C1 (x, y) satisfies conditions presented by the first definition. In addition, C1 (x, y) has the following attributes (Robinson, 1962):

(1) The occurrence of x or y does not depend on someone's observations at all.
(2) C1 (x, y) depends on more things than environments immediately surrounding x and y.
(3) Consequently, C1 (x, y) is a completely objective set.

Here, "does not depend on someone's observations at all" presented in (1) signifies that the first definition is a completely objective regulation, with cognitive subjects either being completely excluded from or having no influence whatever on C1. In addition, the "environments immediately surrounding x and y" in (2) signifies the "present" states of objects. However, because it does not depend on specific observers in accordance with (1), C1 (x, y) becomes a set encompassing not only the past and the present but also the future. Consequently, C1 (x, y) is more comprehensive than environments restricted by current subjectivity. In addition, because of premises (1) and (2), the conclusion (3) that C1 (x, y) is an objective set is derived.

Next, when elements constituting C2 are established as ordered pairs (x, y) and sets of these ordered pairs are established as C2 (x, y), C2 (x, y) satisfies conditions presented by the second definition. In addition, C2 (x, y) has the following attributes:

(1) The occurrence of x or y is observed by someone.
(2) Other specific events of types identical to x and y have been observed previously.

    (3) + (2) ⇒ There is a tendency to transit from ideas about the occurrence of events that are similar to x to those about the occurrence of events that are similar to y and from ideas about the occurrence of events that are similar to x to expectations of the occurrence of events that are similar to y.

(3) It is possible to discern C2 (x, y) from environments immediately surrounding x and y. Consequently, the second definition is essentially determined by attributes defined from the perspective of mental phenomena (Robinson, 1962).

Analysis of C2 presupposes observers. This is the decisive reason why these two definitions differ from each other. Because it is a description of the generation of impressions and ideas, C2 can be seen as a description of mental aspects. Cognitive subjects or observers are therefore presupposed. Consequently, definitions of cause come to be subjective, making it possible to discern C2 (x, y) from the "environments immediately surrounding x and y" because environments restricting cognitive subjects have intervened.

Consequently, the first and second definitions differ from each other in meaning. This is because C1 represents all objective objects from which observers have been excluded while C2 refers to subjective objects presupposing observers. As a result, these two definitions differ in both connotation (intension) and elements of their respective sets. They differ in denotation (extension) as well. In conclusion, according to Robinson, these two definitions differ in both denotation and connotation. They present disparate statements. The first definition represents regularity. It is the correct definition of cause. However, the second definition represents the process of psychological operations. It cannot be seen as a definition. Positivists like Robinson have argued that Hume's first definition of cause only enumerates objective regularity without involving cognitive subjectivity at all. They have pointed out that this can lead to differences in sets constituting the first and second definitions and in denotation in the end.

Regarding C1, Hume pointed out that diverse examples of similar connections, although originally separate and not coming together anywhere except in the mind, could lead one to opinions about abilities or necessity because the mind observed them and gathered ideas (Hume, 1978: 165). "Diverse examples of similar connections" were not cases occurring in a limited location. Originating from completely disparate locations, they gathered solely in the mind because of similarities. Connections of similar cases referred to none other than necessary connections of C1. The location in which they gathered was the *mind*. Consequently, because C1 presupposed cognitive subjectivity according to Hume, ideas about causes and effect were originated from experience and experience informed one that causes and effect were consistently conjoined (Hume, 1978: 89–90). Without presupposing experience, causation could not exist either. Experience presupposed cognitive subjectivity. Experience that excluded subject was meaningless.

Positivists' efforts to establish the two definitions as disparate were erroneous. They excluded cognitive subjectivity from C1 and presupposed cognitive subjectivity for C2, thus making the two yield different denotations. Like C2, C1 is a definition that presupposes cognitive subjectivity. This does not lead to different denotations of the two definitions. Consequently, the key issue is whether C1 is an objective condition or a subjective one. If Hume had set C1 as an objective condition, differences in denotation from C2 described under that subjective condition would have arisen, thus making it difficult to say that these two definitions were definitions of a single concept. The question is: What Hume intended as the condition of C1? From a positivistic perspective, C1 may seem like an objective condition. However, Hume did not stipulate that C1 was a completely objective condition excluding cognitive subjects. Rather, he held an opposite view.

Smith has the position that, in causation, there must exist among objects not only priority in time, proximity in space, and necessary connections, but also inevitable associations (Smith, 1949). Consequently, with C1 alone which only represents simple enumeration of repeated cases, inevitable impressions cannot be yielded even if relations of necessary connections appear to be there. Consequently, C1 is not an appropriate definition for causation. However, C2 is different. In Smith's view, the substance of inevitable association lies in the human mind. This is because C2 refers to internal impressions of necessity. Consequently, Smith sees C2 as an appropriate definition of causation.

Seeing both C1 and C2 as violating Hume's semantic theory, Stroud disapproves both definitions (Stroud, 1978). In other words, for all ideas to have actual meaning, impressions that temporally precede those ideas must be discovered. However, such impressions are found in neither definition. Stroud's critique was that, because C1 only exhibited repeated examples where a single event brought about other events, they were not inevitable impressions. Therefore, mental determination of C2 likewise was only a vague and subjective feeling regarding necessity.

On the other hand, citing the fact that Hume claimed the existence of solely one efficient cause (Hume, 1978: 171), certain scholars have argued that cause includes the only type of necessity instead of logical necessity (Gotterbarn, 1971). In addition, necessary connections and mental determination are presented as conditions of necessity. Stating that one would only have simple coincidence if these two conditions were to be eliminated from causation, Hume therefore approved of C1 and C2, which included these two conditions as appropriate definitions. However, such arguments only present elements of necessity. They do not address inevitable impressions, thus being distant from Hume's semantic theory.

In Millican's view, necessity is the essence of causation. This is revealed by the two definitions of cause (Millican, 2009). According to Millican, causal systems are obtained by reading meaning into the world. They are objective instead of being subjective because they are formed by understanding (Hume, 1978: 149). When necessary connections of objects are observed, judgments are systematically spread and an objective position is read into causation (Hume, 1978: 167). In other words, based on repeated experience in C1, it is possible to guess the effect solely from impressions of the cause in C2, which agrees with Hume's semantic theory of ideas stemming from impressions (Hume, 1975: 294). In addition, C1 serves as the standard of priority in time, proximity in space, and necessary connections. However, it is difficult to say that such an explanation that C1 serves only as the standard for C2 where impressions of necessary connections emerge can properly interpret necessity meant by Hume.

Differences in opinion occur in interpreting these two definitions because of disparate premises regarding what Hume called "necessity." He defined necessity as efficacy, action, capacity, force, internal impressions of the mind, determination of thought, and habitual transference (Hume, 1978: 157–166). However, he stated that impressions of force could not be found in the object world. Consequently, impressions of force can be discovered by repeatedly observing manifestations of connections between cause and effect.

The mind observes diverse examples similarly connected and combines individual ideas. Necessity is a result of such observations and an internal impression of the mind (Hume, 1978: 165). Because Hume stipulated internal impressions of the mind as a necessity, he did not distinguish between actual necessity and inevitable impressions. In other words, internal impressions of the mind (patterns of emotions such as desire, hatred, hope, and fear) were seen as necessity. Because emotions are the mind's reactions, necessity as Hume defined it was a type of reaction from the mind. However, not all mind's reactions could be seen as necessity. Otherwise, even ideal associations stemming from relations of simple similarities among objects would also have to be necessary. Consequently, for Hume, necessity was a mental preference always giving rise to specific mental reactions under specific conditions. Here, "specific conditions" meant temporally preceding and being spatially proximate to objects and having such relations consistently connected (C1). In addition, "specific mental preference" was mental determination manifested by specific conditions (C2).

According to Hume, essential components of necessity were constant unions and the inference of the mind (Hume, 1978: 400). When necessity is thus stipulated, it becomes possible to rebut the argument from Smith and Stroud regarding the absence of necessity in C1. This is because the presence of necessity in C1 is satisfied by the presence of necessary connections among objects alone. Because efficiency originates from necessary connections between two objects, the cause in question is effective when such connections exist. Without these necessary connections, cause of any kind cannot exist (Hume, 1978: 171).

The only condition giving rise to mental determination is necessary connections among objects. Consequently, C1 "functionally" implies C2 while C2 "functionally" presupposes C1. The expression "functionally" is used here because the relation between these two definitions is interrelated within the scope of experience rather than being logical. When it enters cognitive subjectivity, the state of affairs called C1 always and empirically entails the state of affairs called C2. This is because necessary connections described in C1 are "sole" elements of mental determination described in C2 and consequent production of necessity. When examined under such a relation, C1 and C2 are denotatively equivalent. Consequently, C1 bears necessity because there are necessary connections among objects. Therefore, it becomes a reasonable definition of cause. With C1, necessity does not rise to the surface.

In the end, to Hume, necessity referred to cognitive subjects feeling inevitable impressions which were expectations manifested by specific conditions (priority in time, proximity in space, and necessary connections). If one were to impute certain abilities or inevitable associations to objects, one would never be able to observe inevitable associations in objects. One must derive ideas about inevitable associations from what one felt inside (Hume, 1978: 169). These are not impressions of necessity discussed above but are ideas about conscious necessity. This is because impressions of necessity are internal impressions of the mind. They consist of being conscious of and sensing internal impressions of the mind. However, this consciousness does not remain a mere feeling. Instead, it is a cognitive activity where judicative operations of understanding intervene. By regulating necessity ideas, Hume's semantic theory that ideas must stem from impressions preceding them in time can be satisfied in C2.

In the history of early modern philosophy, Hume's theory of causation is important because the time in which he lived was dominated by Descartes' rationalistic worldview. The important question at the time was the idea of substance. Inquiring into it required one to consider absolute rationality and the existence of God. In Hume's view, however, doing so only brought about philosophical ambiguity because these notions had neither been proven nor disproven. To address this issue, he engaged in philosophical groundwork on his own which included the definition of cause as well. In the end, Hume, who espoused thorough empiricism, turned his attention to cognitive subjects instead of the objective world in order to explain concepts not subsumed by experience. Through his unique study of humanism, he strove to derive from laws like those of natural sciences, as had Newton, his contemporary (Hume, 1975: 54–55). The term "necessity" that he used can also be understood in terms of his naturalistic attitude. In science, identical results continuously yielded by experiments are accepted as natural laws. If the same holds true for philosophy, then such repeated results are "inevitable" manifestations of human mental operations. Of course, the "necessity" that Hume spoke of was not inevitability in a logical sense but was the nature of causation as judged by human understanding.

David Hume defined cause as proximity in space, priority in time, and necessary connections from an empirical perspective. In other words, he argued that an object could be called a cause when it preceded, and was proximate to another object, and always yielded a particular reaction under a particular condition. In addition, Hume saw causal pathways between agents' actions and results inductively inferred and the law of cause and effect as acquiring validity owing to its function of explaining events. These were termed inferences to the best explanation. Here, Hume saw cognitive subjects' creation of inevitable impressions under the particular condition mentioned above as the fundamental nature of causal relations judged by human understanding, thus creating a point of connection between objective judgments from facts and normative judgments.

2.2.3 Causation in the Philosophy of Law

Causation has not been a principal realm within the philosophy of law. Regardless, Hart and Honore's book "Causation in the Law" is a thorough and scholarly study of the concept of causation in Anglo-American law (Hart & Honoré, 1985). Closely reasoned with full reference to the literature and a considerable treatment of continental theories, the book contains a serious attempt to restate the law in tort, contract, and crime in an intelligible way (Calabresi, 1975). Hart and Honore dealt with two basic questions. First, they dealt with whether and to what extent causation in legal contexts differs from causation outside the law such as in science or everyday life. Second, they dealt with what are appropriate criteria in law for deciding whether one action or event has caused another harmful event. The importance of these questions is that responsibility in law often depends on showing that a specific action or event or state of affairs has caused specific harm or loss to another. Based on these concepts of Hart and Honore, this chapter covers the nature and functions of causation in the philosophy of law, the relationship between causation and legal responsibility, and the criteria for the existence of a causal connection in law (Hart & Honoré, 1985: 9–12). This chapter focuses on causes-in-fact and the proximate cause requirement (causally relevant conditions and grounds for limiting responsibility).

Initially, a theory on how causal notions should function in different contexts is required. This is because law is concerned with the application of causal ideas embodied in the language of statutes and decisions to particular situations. In the context of application, the notion of cause is a multi-purpose, functional tool. One forward-looking and perhaps fundamental function of causation is that it specifies what will happen and by what stages if certain conditions are present together. This function serves to provide an idea of a causal process. Another function of causation from the perspective of backward-looking and explanatory is that it shows which earlier conditions best account for some later event or state of affairs. In addition, causation is attributive. It determines the extent of responsibility of agents for outcomes that follow on their agency or their intervention in the world (Hart & Honoré, 1985: 62–83).

Many legal inquiries have attempted to explain how some event or state of affairs arose, especially an untoward event such as death or a state of affairs such as insolvency. However, whether someone is liable to punishment, to pay compensation, or is entitled to claim compensation often depends on whether the person who is potentially liable or entitled has caused harm of a sort that the law seeks to avoid. For example, all systems of law hold that a person can be guilty of homicide only if he or she has caused another's death. It is a civil wrong to cause injury to another by negligence in driving a vehicle. However, the claim can be barred or reduced if the negligent conduct of the injured person is also a cause of the injury. When rules of law attributing responsibility for harm are formulated in statutes, regulations, and judicial decisions, the word *cause* is often used. The notion that a causal connection between agency and harm must be established is often implied, even when the word *cause* is not used. For example, a verb such as *damage* implies a causal relation between an agency and the harm done. In legal contexts, the possible range of agency is not confined to human conduct. It can be extended to damage done by the agency of juristic persons, animals, inanimate objects such as motor vehicles, and inanimate forces such as fire.

In all such instances, the notion of cause is central to legal inquiry. To establish responsibility, it must be shown that the harm was done or brought about by the agency that the law deems to be the potential basis for the existence or extent of liability (Hart & Honoré, 1985: 62–67). However, the relationship between causing harm and legal responsibility is complex. Such complexities include the incidence of responsibility, grounds of responsibility, items between which causal connection must be demonstrated, and a variety of relationships that can be regarded as causal in some sense. With regard to the grounds of responsibility, for a person to cause harm or loss to another in law is neither a necessary nor sufficient condition of being legally responsible for the harm. The risk may be voluntarily assumed, as in insurance contracts, or may be imposed by law, as in the case of an employer's liability for wrongs committed by employees in the course of their employment. Therefore, in law, the main grounds of responsibility for harm are an agent's personal responsibility for causing harm and a person's responsibility arising from the fact that he, she, or it bears the risk of having to answer in legal proceedings for the harm in question.

Causing harm is not a necessary condition for legal responsibility as there are many contexts in which a person is civilly or criminally responsible, irrespective of whether harm has been caused by their conduct or by an agency for which they are responsible (Hart & Honoré, 1985: 109–113). Both inside and outside the law, many actions are regarded as wrongful whether or not they cause tangible harm. Moreover, the imposition of penalties in civil law and punishments in criminal law do not need to bear any relation to the harm caused by the conduct for which the penalty or punishment is imposed. A further complication concerns the items between which a causal connection must be shown to exist in law. The events in issue must be identified not only from the points of view of the time, place, and persons involved, but also from the aspect of the events between which a causal link must be specified in such a way as to show that it falls within the relevant legal categories, such as negligence and physical injury.

In the context of interpersonal relationships, legal responsibility is imposed on those who influence others by advising, encouraging, helping, permitting, coercing, deceiving, misinforming, or providing opportunities to others that motivate or enable them to act in a way that is harmful to themselves or others. The existence of such a wide spectrum of causal or near-causal grounds of responsibility recognized in law and morality raises the question of whether any uniform theory of causation is capable of accounting for all such grounds (Hart & Honoré, 1985: 62–67). Theories concerning the criteria for the existence of a causal connection in law fall into two types. The first concerns the identification of causally relevant conditions of an outcome or in the language of causal minimalists, i.e., cause-in-fact (Malone, 1956). The cause is evaluated to be a necessary condition (i.e., *sine qua none*), a sufficient condition, or a necessary member of a set of conditions that are together sufficient for the outcome (Hart & Honoré, 1985: 109–113). The cause is necessary or sufficient in particular circumstances in issue. The second type of theory concerns the criteria for determining the limits of legal responsibility for causing harm. This is because, even supposing that the alleged cause constitutes the right sort of condition of the outcome such as a necessary condition, responsibility, cannot extend indefinitely (Hart & Honoré, 1985: 122–127).

We strive to set a type of condition that can be attributed to an agency for its action or intervention to count as causal. This sometimes requires that all limiting factors be brought under a single umbrella such as "proximate cause" or "adequate cause," even though there are a number of distinct reasons for imposing limits on the extent of responsibility underlying these phrases (Hart & Honoré, 1985: 32–50). An intervention such as human action may be necessary to the outcome, i.e., a *but-for* condition, and the intervention must form a necessary part of complex conditions that are sufficient for the outcome. With regard to causally relevant conditions, cause-in-fact is divided into a substantial factor and a contributor to the outcome. The *but-for* theory endorsed by many legal and philosophical theorists has heuristic advantage that a simple and often reliable way of ruling out the existence of a causal connection between agency and harm is to ask whether the harm would have occurred in the absence of the agency. However, there are cases in which the *but-for* test is difficult to reconcile with an intuitive judgment of responsibility.

Difficult legal problems can arise in certain cases of over-determination often termed as overtaking causes or causal preemption (Hart & Honoré, 1985: 84–87). Suppose that a lethal dose of poison is given. However, the victim is fatally wounded before the poison takes effect. The pre-empting, not the pre-empted condition, is taken to be the cause of death. Which condition is taken to preempt the other is sometimes controversial, but it is clearer than reaching a decision. Attention must be paid to the stages and processes by which the alleged causes lead to the harmful outcome. Whichever cause is favored has to be applied in support of the law's commitment to vindicating rights and securing a fair distribution of risks.

With regard to proximate cause, limiting theories are invoked because if every causally relevant condition such as cause-in-fact is treated as a grounding responsibility for the outcomes to which it is causally relevant, then the extent of legal responsibility will extend almost indefinitely (Hart & Honoré, 1985: 28–50). Theories in question, therefore, embody reasons for limiting the extent of legal responsibility. However, the reasons adduced for limiting responsibility are differently viewed by various theorists. Causal minimalists treat all these theories as non-causal in the sense that they embody grounds of legal policy other than holding an agent responsible for the harm caused by their action or intervention (Moore, 2009). Certain theorists reject causal minimalism because it involves a restricted notion of cause that is not current in an extra-legal context (Hart & Honoré, 1985: 95–108). They propose grounds of limitation reflecting the type of causal judgements that would be made outside of the law. The chief grounds proposed are that responsibility is limited when a later intervention of a certain type is a condition of the harmful outcome and/or when the agency has not substantially increased the probability of a harmful outcome that in fact supervenes.

The limitations set by the purposes of legal rules cannot be regarded as causal. They vary from one branch of the law or one legal system to another. It is true that sometimes the purpose of a legal prohibition may be the simple one of imposing responsibility for the harm caused by a breach of that prohibition (Hart & Honoré, 1985: 84–87). In that case, the limits set by causal and purposive criteria coincide. Even in such a case, it is a matter of legal policy to determine which types of harm are to be compensated or lead to criminal liability. Therefore, purposive limits on responsibility either have to be regarded as additional to those proposed by those who reject causal minimalism or as replacement (Moore, 2009).

Although foreseeability bears some relation to probability, it is clearly a non-causal criterion. One can apply it only to human conduct, not to other alleged causes. Moreover, some supporters of risk theory suggest that different criteria should govern the existence and extent of legal liability (Stapleton, 2001). Even if foreseeability of harm is a condition of liability, principles of risk allocation are placed on the agent who is at fault in failing to foresee and take precautions against harm. There is a risk that an unforeseeable harm will result from an agent's fault provided that the harm is of a type that the rule of law in question seeks to prevent. There is no reason to suppose that the law, when it engages in explanatory inquiries, will adopt different criteria of causation from those employed outside the law such as those in physical and social sciences or in everyday life. However, requirements of proof may lead to a divergence, even here, for example, between what would medically be treated as the cause of a disease and what would count in law as its cause.

2.3 Causation in Criminal Law

Legal norms simultaneously evaluate human actions as appraisal norms and induce desirable human actions as decisional norms. Likewise, criminal law is an appraisal norm and a decisional norm at the same time. Consequently, criminal law becomes a rule regarding actions by prohibiting or ordering citizens regarding the performance of particular actions. Criminal law as an appraisal norm clarifies which actions are criminal actions contravening criminal law and as a decisional norm enables citizens to judge which actions constitute criminal actions (Honig, 1995: 19–20). A key requirement for imposing penal responsibilities, causation suppresses causing actions (e.g., stabling someone with a knife) with respect to results that are prohibited in criminal law (e.g., causing someone to die). Here, if and when punishments imposed by law courts are accepted as the minimal morality and ethics that the defendants should have upheld, validity is conferred on the execution of penalties. A regulation on causation, Article 17 of the South Korean Criminal Act stipulates that when any action is not linked to the occurrence of danger, which is an element of crime, the results are not to entail punishments. While the position regarding this that is supported by the majority is the *theory of objective imputation*, there has been legal wrangling regarding the interpretation of the concept of *acceptable risks* or an *increase in risks*. Consequently, discussions on this are necessary in terms of both legal hermeneutics and the unity of the criminal law system. In particular, because one of the purposes of law is to prevent disputes, necessary is problem-focused thinking that seeks appropriate solutions to specific issues. It is necessary also for the theory of causation to integrate these two ways of thinking and to engage in rational discussions through practical reason. However, system-focused discussions have hitherto been dominant. Consequently, discussing points of contention surrounding the theory of objective imputation in criminal law through cases of criminal trials will be useful for examining legal causation.

2.3.1 Theory of Objective Imputation and Criticisms

Although the dominant theory in German criminal jurisprudence at present is the theory of objective imputation, the theory of adequate causation (i.e., *Adäquanztheorie*) and relevance theory (i.e., *Relevanztheorie*), too, continue to receive support (Roxin, 1995). So-called indispensable and essential actions (i.e., *conditio sine qua non*) are acknowledged when a lawful relationship between them and the results have been realized. According to the theory of objective imputation, the objective possibility for causation to be effected between causing actions and damages depends on whether or not the actions performed by the individuals in question have created risks constituting a legally important body of the crime (i.e., *corpus delicti*) (Kaufmann, 1995a: 192). However, the possibility of the occurrence of dangerous results is distinguished from causation in the natural sciences. This is because crime committed by omission is seen as having a functional relationship of responsibility with results due to the failure to perform duties that should have been fulfilled and therefore punished (Lampe, 1995: 108–131). Consequently, legal causation is closely related to the reasoning procedures of lawsuits and has been carefully discussed with a focus mainly on criminal negligence, false omission (i.e., *unechte Unterlassung*), and overlapped causation (i.e., *Doppelkausalität*). First, criminal negligence is causal responsibility presumed in cases where agents have violated their duty of care within their dominant scope and given rise to foreseeable damages or risks. Next, false omission arises in situations where (1) individuals with the intentional obligations to prevent the occurrence of dangers (2) who were capable of taking actions and (3) who were solely able to prevent dangers (4) committed nonfeasance, and (5) that nonfeasance is evaluated to be identical to feasance in the results (Honig, 1995: 19–20; Kaufmann, 1995a: 192). For reference, crime committed by omission refers to the occurrence of preventable results because those with intentional obligations were passive and did not perform legally demanded actions. Consequently, when seen from the perspective of objective imputation, causation between *nonfeasance* and the *results* is acknowledged for false omission in accordance with the two standards of hypothetical causation (i.e., *hypothetische Kausalität*) and risk realization (i.e., *Risikorealisierung*) (Kaufmann, 1995b: 80–92; Ulsenheimer, 1995: 212–215). Finally, in terms of the actual avoidability of the results, overlapped causation confirms causation through normative evaluations.

Although the theory of objective imputation is the currently dominant theory in Germany, it has specified the body of the crime of causation only to the extent that agents' actions must have created legally criticizable dangers before the occurrence of the results and have been realized as actual dangers, and there are many interpretative problems (Kaufmann, 1995b: 80–92). In particular, it fails to provide fundamental answers to the question of why increasing risks as a result of actions is illegal. Moreover, objective imputation is not the only criterion in circumstances precluding wrongfulness such as self-defense. In other words, this is merely an element in evaluating self-responsibility (i.e., *Eigenverantwortung*), acceptable risks, body of the crime, and illegality. Consequently, the theory of objective imputation has nearly no implications for intentional offenses and is quite difficult to apply to actual issues in the case of criminal negligence as well because its criteria of imputation are too abstract and normative (Ulsenheimer, 1995: 212–215).

2.3.2 Comparison with the Anglo-American Theory of Causation

When the similarities and differences between the theory of objective imputation and the Anglo-American theory of causation are compared, they are as follows. First, both theories have the same basic framework in distinguishing between factual causation and normative causation and performing evaluations by each stage. The method of reviewing fact relevance first and then discussing legal causation in the Anglo-American theory of causation corresponds to the theory of objective imputation, which determines causation through normative evaluations according to the conditional theory. Next, substantiality, dangerousness, possibility of expectation to legal acts, and substantiality of intervening causes presented by the Anglo-American theory of causation are similar to objective dominance, fore-knowledge possibility, acceptable risks, and increase in risks in the theory of objective imputation. Finally, specific judgments on causation are left to judicial precedents in the UK and the USA, and Germany similarly does not have stipulated or statutory regulations on causation, thus leaving specific judgments to theories and judicial precedents.

However, there are the following fundamental differences between the two as well. First, the theory of objective imputation is a theory derived from system-focused thinking, while the Anglo-American theory of causation originates from problem-focused thinking. The theory of objective imputation establishes a higher concept of *objective imputation* and presents the criteria of *risk creation*, *risk realization*, and *protective purpose of norms* below. On the contrary, as for the Anglo-American theory of causation, law courts have judged sensible and appropriate causation in specific cases from a problem-focused perspective and accumulated judicial precedents over a prolonged period. Moreover, the theory of objective imputation constitutes deductive thinking in that it establishes *objective imputation* as a higher concept and derives elements of individual imputation from it. However, the UK and the USA are based on inductive thinking in that law courts review similarities in specific cases according to precedents and apply them. Because scholars classify individual cases and interpret them after placing them in contextual frameworks, this is an *abductive* inference format (Danermark, Ekstrom, Jakobsen, & Karlsson, 2005: 41–70). Here, *abductive* is the opposite of *retroductive*, where conditions that serve as the grounds of specific phenomena are reconstructed from descriptions and analyses of those phenomena. Second, the Anglo-American theory of causation has been formed through judicial precedents, and the common sense and experiences of the public have accumulated to function as decisional norms in daily life. However, the theory of objective imputation is a theory of the pursuit of study. Consequently, distinguishing between the theory of objective imputation and the Anglo-American theory of causation is very useful and necessary for interpreting Article 17 of the South Korean Criminal Act.

2.3.3 Application to the South Korean Criminal Act

In relation to the interpretation of Article 17 of the Criminal Act, judicial precedents and theories have been divided, with the former supporting the theory of proximate causal relations and the latter supporting both the theory of objective imputation and the theory of proximate causal relations. Unlike its German counterpart, the South Korean Criminal Act (Article 17) has legal provisions about causation and therefore makes somewhat different judgments regarding causation. Nevertheless, the theory of objective imputation is the majority opinion in the laws in both countries. This theory is supported in South Korea largely for three reasons. First, while the association between actions and results can be judged in terms of the association with natural law based on experience, jurisprudence needs standards for judging the matter of responsibility among agents because it is a discipline that addresses normative value judgments (Roxin, 1995: 48–49). Second, guidelines for resolving specific issues in terms of lawyering are necessary because the concepts of substantiality and the possibility of foreknowledge are helpful. Third, because the crimes of omission do not have actual effects, whereby changes are brought about externally, in the theory of objective imputation, causation in the sense of the natural sciences does not exist, and only the *performance of intentional obligations*, the logical relationship between hypothetical actions and results, is determined. In other words, in order to impose responsibilities in criminal law on crimes of omission, the causation between nonfeasance and the occurrence of the results must be evaluated only on a normative level. Likewise, if there were no accessory actions in cases of accessory offenders, the results of principal offenders would not occur, and if legally prohibited dangers increase through the accessory actions in question, objective imputation is affected.

However, there is criticism that the criteria of imputation presented by the theory of objective imputation are abstract and normative. First, the requirements of risk creation presented by this theory demand comprehensive judgments and therefore are unclear, and judgments on *danger* in terms of the principle of increase in danger, too, are difficult. Consequently, there is also criticism that, when seen in terms of the protective purpose of norms, actual significance of the contributions of the theory of objective imputation to the elucidation of causation is minimal besides the role of referring to existing legal principles. Second, it is still controversial whether or not, unlike in the theory of proximate causal relations, the association between the actions and results of crime committed by omission can be seen not as a natural or logical relationship but as an issue of imputation to impose responsibility on agents. This is because, from the naturalistic perspective, according to which cause is force, attributable reasons are imposed on the outside world even though it has not performed any causal intervention. Such logic expands even to the position that the intention of crime committed by omission cannot be acknowledged as an efficient cause in accordance with René Descartes' mind–body dualism. At the time, causal interactions intersecting the disparate spheres of body and mind were impossible. However, contemporary cognitive science has elucidated through electroencephalograms, magnetic resonance imaging (MRI), positron emission tomography (PET), and functional magnetic resonance imaging (fMRI) how human brain nerves affect physical layers. Consequently, applying the theory of objective imputation to crime committed by omission is still controversial. Third, the theory of objective imputation is too system-oriented despite the advantage that it presents to the public the correct rules of action. Consequently, it is deficient in its understanding of human actions' object orientation in the actual life world and is abstract when applied as an empirical criterion or regulation that can predict the responsibilities for actions through categorical evaluations.

2.3.4 Legal Cases in Korea

The causation issue can be examined through classic cases of intentional offense and criminal negligence as follows. In the first case, five people, including the assailant A, attacked the victims' heads and bodies with iron pipes and square bars and stabbed their arms with sickles.[1] Although they may not have given the victims fatal wounds, the victims were hospitalized. A victim was treated for acute renal failure caused by a punctured wound but developed complications including septicemia and disseminated intravascular coagulation. The victim should have restricted his fluid intake considering that he had a very low level of urine output, but because he ate food such as cola and gimbap recklessly, he died of water retention within his body. On this case, the Supreme Court judged that since the act of homicide does not have to be the singular and direct cause to the result of the victim's death, the causation between the act of homicide and the victim's death can be established. Such was the case despite the fact that another fact has intervened in the relation and also served as the direct cause of death, since the consequences could be conventionally anticipated.

In the aforementioned case, the victim himself was the conductor of the intervention. First, in terms of factual causation, the conditional relation between the harmful acts of the assailants and the victim's death can be established. Second, in terms of normative causation, by putting the objective circumstances during the

---

[1] The Decision of the Supreme Court of Korea 93Do3612 (1994. 3. 22.)

conduct, that is, the degree of violence induced by the assailants and the stabbing by using a sickle, one can reach to the conclusion of the victim's death. In regard to the substantiality of the intervening cause, the intervention of the victim himself, that is, the fact that he developed complications after eating cola and gimbap, cannot be considered more substantially serious than the assailants' act of violence. The Supreme Court ruled that the victim's intervention is *something that can be anticipated* but it would be more reasonable to rule that the fact that the victim could die due to the assailants' conduct is predictable in terms of the substantiality of the intervening cause, rather than considering the victim's intervention as something that can be conventionally predicted by the assailants.

In the second case in which the defendant A, while driving a motorcycle, hit the victim B, who was jaywalking, after 40–60 s of which a truck ran over the victim B who was unconscious on the road and killed him, the Supreme Court ruled that there is a proximate causal relation between the two parties on the grounds that the defendant A hit the victim B by being negligent in taking note of one's surroundings and that when putting the traffic situation in the nighttime in consideration, if the possibility of the victim being run over by drivers of following vehicles who are even slightly negligent of their surroundings during the 60 s the victim B is left unconscious on the road can be anticipated, the defendant A's negligent driving becomes the direct cause to the death of the victim B.[2]

First, in terms of factual causation, a conditional relationship exists between A's conduct and B's death according to the empirical criterion stating that B's death would not have occurred if not for A's conduct, by which factual causation can be accepted. Second, in terms of normative causation, considering that the objective situation surrounding the accident, that is, the fact that B, when abandoned in the nighttime, can be run over by other vehicles, had been anticipated, and assuming that the truck driver's negligence is less serious than that of A's, normative causation can be accepted between B's conduct and the consequences of his act of accidental (unpremeditated) homicide. In this case, the Supreme Court found causation with only an objective possibility of expectation of legality to act as a criterion. However, normative causation should have been considered through the objective possibility of foreknowledge and the substantiality of the intervening case after examining the conditional relationship with factual causation, as judgment solely based on the objective possibility of foreknowledge will leave the argument of normative causation weak. According to the theory of objective imputation, a decision is based on risk creation, risk realization, and the protective purpose of norms. Such criteria, however, can be difficult for the conductor to understand at the time of the conduct. Furthermore, it is unclear whether these criteria differ from the purposive evaluation of norms which apply to cases of negligence.

---

[2]The Decision of the Supreme Court of Korea 90Do580 (1990. 5. 22.)

2.3.5   Remarks

Article 17 of the Criminal Act stipulates, "Any act which is not connected with the danger which is an element of a crime, it shall not be punishable for the results." "Any act... for the results" bespeaks the fact relevance that must exist between actions and results, and there are no differences among various theories regarding this. However, there is legal wrangling among theories with respect to the interpretation of *any act which is not connected with the danger which is an element of a crime*. This is interpreted as *objective danger* by those who support the theory of proximate causal relations and as *objective imputation* by those who support the theory of objective imputation, respectively. According to socially accepted ideas, *danger* refers to a state that is proximate to harm based on empirical knowledge. According to common opinions, danger consists of probability (i.e., *Wahrscheinlichkeit*) and harmfulness (*Schädlichkeit*), which, combined, are considered the "possibility of infringing on rights" in the future. Consequently, the theory of proximate causal relations judges that if and when actions are appropriate for actually giving rise to the results, the danger of infringing on rights exists within the results of the performance of such actions. In other words, the "[occurrence of] danger" in Article 17 of the Criminal Act is the *possibility of the occurrence of infringements on rights*, and normative standards such as *substantiality* in the theory of adequate causation can be applied (Roxin, 1995: 48–49). Legal provisions must be understood interdependently through logical, historical, and teleological interpretations. However, the standard for interpreting law is the objective volition of the legislators, as is apparent from legal provisions. Consequently, despite the fact that theories and judicial precedents in South Korea have already embraced the theory of adequate causation at the time of the enactment of the Criminal Act, it still cannot be said that Article 17 must be understood via the concept of *danger* in the theory of adequate causation. In other words, understanding *danger* here as the danger of infringing on rights accords with the objective volition of legislators. Causation signifies the description possibility of issues, proximity, and association, while in the social sciences, whose objects are human actions, causation is a probable relationship that is realized when hypotheses and prerequisites have been fulfilled. The principle of cause and effect must be a principle that provides comprehensive *explanations* of objects such as phenomena, obtaining validity through its *explanatory functions*. Consequently, danger in Article 17 of the Criminal Act includes the meanings of the *objective possibility of expectation to legal acts* and *substantiality* and cannot truly be interpreted as adopting the position of the theory of proximate causal relations when interpreted teleologically.

Causation in criminal law is classified into fact relevance and normative relations. Judgments must be made first through factual causation and according to experience rules, and normative evaluations must then be performed according to the purposiveness of human motives and actions. At the same time, laws explaining causation must be comprehensible and predictable to agents. Although judgments in accordance with empirical rules are based on factual relations, judgments of the purposiveness of human actions must be addressed in relation to normative causal relations. For example, judging whether a criminal defendant's intended action led to predictable results or if a rupture arises in causal relations due to elements such as the action of a third party can be a question in criminal policy. These types of questions form the reason behind the support of what is termed the theory of objective imputation, according to which no act is to be punished for its results when it is not connected to the occurrence of danger, which is an element of crime, in terms of criminal law. This helps to determine the matter of the responsibility of agents in criminal law, which requires normative value judgments through the concept of substantiality or the possibility of foreknowledge. When the criteria for imputation are abstract and normative, dangers cannot be determined easily, and when crimes of omission are considered, it is difficult logically to connect the imputation of responsibility.

The present chapter of this study has reviewed the Anglo-British theory of causation, which approaches causation from problem-focused thinking, through Article 17 of the Criminal Act. Simultaneously an appraisal norm and a decisional norm, causation must be established as citizens' everyday norm over a considerably prolonged period through judicial precedents. Consequently, it is necessary to review how the criteria of causation are applied to judicial precedents and to derive legal principles on causation that are sensible and appropriate for the objectives of norms.

2.4 Causation in Civil Law

2.4.1 Causation in Medical Malpractices

For claims for damages to be acknowledged in civil law, legally significant factual causation must exist (Kim, 2016).[3] When direct violence consecutively gives rise to succeeding damages, liability for damages is established in terms of the extent to which causation is to be legally acknowledged. The causation demanded by liability for default (non-performance of obligations; Article 390) and liability for illegal acts (torts; Article 750) in the South Korean Civil Act is factual causation (Jee, 2014: 1356–1369). As for compensation for damages due to default, general damages are the limits, and as for damages due to special circumstances, debtors have liability for compensation only when they were aware of those circumstances (Article 393).

In South Korea's Damage Compensation Act, the position of both the majority theory and judicial precedents regarding legal causation is that of the theory of proximate causal relations, which acknowledges liability for compensation to causal relations having substantiality. The majority theory only evaluates the

---

[3]The Decision of the Supreme Court of Korea 99Da67147 (2000. 3. 28.)

substantiality of causation, without distinguishing between the establishing requisites of liability for damages and the scope of compensation for damages. However, when determining the presence or absence of causation, legal evaluations presuppose factual causation. This is an indispensable condition for imposing liability for damages on either debtors or assailants with respect to damages that have occurred. As for cases involving compensation for damages due to default, evaluating factual causation between the non-fulfillment of contracts and the occurrence of damages is clear. In addition, even in cases of illegal acts where no contractual relationship whatsoever exists between the persons directly involved, factual causation between violence and the results of damages is clear. Likewise, in medical malpractice cases, there is factual causation between the causing medical actions and the ensuing damages. However, there also exist cases where it is difficult to establish with certainty whether or not damages that have occurred are due to assailants' actions, as in cases of environmental pollution. In particular, in medical malpractice cases, physicians' acts of diagnosis and treatment intervene where patients already have underlying diseases such that the effects of treatments differ according to the individuals' physical predispositions, with unforeseen results occurring as well. Consequently, in many cases, it is difficult to specify that damages are due to medical actions. Moreover, it is difficult to specify the causing actions that have incurred damages because a single act of treatment for a patient includes diverse actions such as injections and the administration of drugs and involves as well the actions of various medical providers.

To evaluate specifically which parts of medical actions constitute actions causing violence or harm, focus is placed on scientific and medical determination. However, because legal evaluations elucidate causing actions in medical lawsuits, normative evaluations that make use of medical knowledge must be conducted (Shin, 2012). Moreover, in medical malpractice lawsuits, factual causation is important because of the issues of the establishment of liability for compensation and the scope of responsibilities (Park, 2002). In establishing the scope of damages, it becomes difficult to determine substantiality when physical reactions differ according to the individual and damages are due to plural contending actions. Consequently, in medical malpractice cases, the scope of compensation for damages adopts the method where once liability for damages is established, all damages that have occurred in the causal chain are to be compensated for.

2.4.2   Objects of Proof and the Burden of Proof

In medical malpractice cases, the objects of proof are the causing medical actions and the damages that have occurred to patients. Consequently, the major fact that physicians' certain acts of treatment have resulted in injuries or death to patients is proven. As for methods to prove this, direct demonstration exists but is not used because it is difficult in medical malpractice cases, and demonstration through indirect facts is used (Shin, 2012).

In medical malpractice cases, the demonstration of compensation for damages demands the demonstration of the existence of causation that will lead to judges' conviction. Consequently, patients, who are the plaintiffs, must prove the existence of causation between medical providers' medical actions and damages so that judges will be convinced of a high degree of probability (Lee, 2016). Although medical malpractice lawsuits demand medical knowledge, demonstration during trials differs from scientific demonstration. However, practical problems occur if and when the general principle that the fact of the existence of causation must be proven to convince judges is applied verbatim to medical malpractice lawsuits. Because patients all differ in physical predispositions and reactions to treatments, the empirical criterion that identical measures lead to identical results does not hold true completely in medical malpractice cases. Consequently, demanding demonstration of the existence of causation to the extent that it will convince judges raises the probability of defeat in lawsuits for the persons directly involved, who bear the burden of proof. Consequently, in light of the intention of compensation systems, which seek to impose damages fairly and validly, medical malpractice cases must relax the degree of demonstration. In fact, many rulings of medical malpractice lawsuits have acknowledged causation with substantial probability alone, instead of a high degree of probability.[4]

2.4.3 Review of Judicial Precedents

2.4.3.1 Rulings Regarding the Interference of Proof

The interference of proof refers to situations where the persons directly involved, who do not bear the burden of proof, make it difficult for the other parties, who do bear the burden of proof, to demonstrate their arguments. When alterations of or omissions from medical records are accompanied by negligence in medical procedures, judicial precedents consider such situations as constituting the interference of proof and evaluate physicians' negligence as having existed during treatment. However, in cases where it is difficult to see negligence with respect to the duty of care as having been committed during medical procedures, the act of interfering with proof is evaluated as not having a great effect on causation. Law courts synthesize diverse facts concerning acts of interfering with proof for each medical accident and evaluate advantages and disadvantages regarding the interference of proof in accordance with free evaluations of evidence. Consequently, medical providers' interference of proof helps to overcome patients' difficulties with demonstration.

---

[4]The Decision of the Supreme Court of Korea 2009Da82275 (2012. 1. 27.); The Decision of the Supreme Court of Korea 2008Da22030 (2009. 12. 10.); The Decision of the Supreme Court of Korea 2004Da52576 (2005. 9. 30.)

2.4.3.2 Violent Presumptions

(1) Law Courts' Violent Presumptions

In medical malpractice lawsuits, a method widely used to acknowledge negligence or causation is that of violent presumptions. After eliminating possible causes of damages one by one, law courts evaluate the last remaining one as the cause of damages. For example, when A, B, and C are facts by which patients may die and D is physicians' surgical actions, because facts A, B, and C do not exist, the remaining D is seen as the cause of death. Through de facto presumptions, patients help to prove causation by presenting specific indirect facts that can result in damages instead of directly specifying and proving causation. For these reasons, the presumption of negligence or causation through de facto presumptions is widely used as a way of mitigating demonstration. In fact, many rulings acknowledge negligence and causation by presuming that, in light of indirect fact A, damage B has been caused by negligence C. Law courts make use of the patterns of event courses by presuming that even in cases where results that should inevitably exist following certain medical actions have not occurred, the results that have thus failed to occur are due to negligence in their causing actions. In addition, facts are presumed by using occurrence frequency or probability as an indirect fact; or causation is presumed by using the temporal proximity between medical actions and damages or the impossibility of the intervention of other causes as the reason. In cases where causal associations are too weak with a single indirect fact alone, law courts make de facto presumptions as well when the probability increases after the combination of numerous indirect facts.

(2) Law Courts' Evaluations of Statistical Probability and Problems

According to judicial precedents, in issues that present statistical probability as an important indirect fact presuming causation, causing actions are seen as the grounds for presuming causation even when their possibility of resulting in damages is not very high. For example, vaccinations are acknowledged as causes of death, with a fatality rate of 0.002% as the basis, and physicians' negligence was acknowledged in cerebral palsy cases, with the possibility of occurrence amounting to 5–7% as the grounds. Of course, along with fatality rates, law courts took into consideration cerebral congestion or submacular hemorrhage that had developed in patients as a possible adverse reaction. In cerebral palsy cases, hypoxic ischemic brain damage that had developed in newborn infants was taken into consideration together with statistical frequency and indirect facts to evaluate causation.[5] However, when the statistical probability of occurrence is low, it is necessary to raise the probability of causation by combining other indirect facts.[6]

---

[5]The Decision of the Supreme Court of Korea 2004Da13045 (2005. 10. 28.)
[6]The Decision of the Supreme Court of Korea 94Da28218 (1994. 4. 14.)

(3) Presumptions by the Non-intervention of Other Causes

When making de facto presumptions through indirect facts, the impossibility of the intervention of other causes must be determined. Examples include the fact that there were no health anomalies before medical actions and judicial precedents where damages have appeared only in areas that received acts of treatment. On the other hand, regarding whether or not negligence is a cause of damage, it is sufficient to prove the existence of acts of medical negligence based on the common sense of the public. Medical malpractice cases use a method by which negligence is acknowledged to have resulted in damage once it has been presumed rather than evaluating causation as regards negligence, the causing action, and the results separately. Consequently, temporal proximity, the identicalness of areas that have undergone surgery and areas in which the results have occurred, and impossibility of the intervention of other causes are requirements for presuming causation. For example, because the areas treated developed side effects immediately after medical procedures and such side effects did not exist before the medical actions such that other causes did not intervene in the occurrence of the side effects, these side effects can be presumed to have been caused by physicians' negligence.

(4) "Demonstration of Negligence Based on the Common Sense of the Public" in Causation Evaluations

As a method for acknowledging de facto causation in cases of medical malpractice, law courts presume causation by making use of the empirical criteria of various indirect facts. Presumptions of causation through indirect facts are realized after the combination of elements such as temporal proximity, probabilistic possibility, and the impossibility of the intervention of other causes. However, because evaluating the presence or absence of negligence remains difficult for patients, law courts acknowledge negligence when there is a "demonstration of negligence based on the common sense of the public," thus reducing the burden of proof on the patient. In evaluations of negligence in actual rulings, the existence of specific types of violations of the duty of care of the physician has been evaluated based on professional medical knowledge.[7] Here, law courts must neither evaluate negligence by mechanical standards nor fail properly to consider the contexts of the issues.

(5) Unclear Standards Regarding the Degree of Probability

In medical malpractice cases, law courts acknowledge statistical probability as a single indirect fact when presumptions of causation are made by using indirect facts. However, there are cases where the grounds for evaluating the degree of probability are unclear because consistent statistical figures are not used as the standards of evaluations. When presuming causation between acts of treatment and serious damages through the impossibility of the intervention of statistical

---

[7]The Decision of the Supreme Court of Korea 2001Da20217 (2003. 11. 27.); The Decision of the Supreme Court of Korea 98Da50586 (2000. 12. 1.); The Decision of the Supreme Court of Korea 99Da3709 (1999. 6. 11.)

probability or other causes, it is undesirable for jurists and the jury to differ in evaluations of the degree of probability. Consequently, in situations where the probability that serious damages to patients have occurred due to physicians' negligence is not high, it is unfair to impose the burden of proof regarding non-negligence on the physicians directly involved.[8]

2.4.4   Remarks

In medical malpractice lawsuits, the acknowledgment of causation is closely tied to determining the negligence of physicians, which constitutes a causing action. Law courts have acknowledged de facto causation when, in accordance with judicial precedents, there is temporal proximity between medical actions and the damage generated, the probability of the occurrence of damage due to medical actions is not too low, and it is difficult to say that causes other than medical actions have intervened. Consequently, whether or not liability for damages is to be imposed on physicians depends on the negligence of the physicians, which is the causing action. However, it is very difficult for patients to prove the presence or absence of negligence in medical actions. Consequently, judicial precedents have presumed negligence and reduced the burden of proof on patients when medical negligence has been demonstrated at the level of common sense of the public. However, because determining violations of the duty of care with respect to medical actions based on professional medical knowledge complicates the granting of relief for victims, the burden of proof for patients must be mitigated such that legal causation can be determined more reasonably.

Civil law addresses the responsibility for default or for illegal acts based on factual causation. Consequently, only factual causation through which claims for compensation for damages can be acknowledged based on the theory of proximate causal relations is determined. However, in medical malpractice lawsuits, it is difficult for patients, who are the plaintiffs, to prove the existence of a causal relationship between their medical providers' medical practices and damages in such a way that judges will be convinced of a high degree of probability. Consequently, in cases such as those where violent presumptions are possible, statistical possibility is high, or causes other than the one in question could not have intervened, the plaintiffs' burden of proof is mitigated.

---

[8]The Decision of the Supreme Court of Korea 2005Da5867 (2007. 5. 31.); The Decision of the Supreme Court of Korea 2002Da45185 (2004. 10. 28.)

2.5 Causation in Epidemiology

In recent lawsuits demanding compensation for damages due to unlawful acts, cases
have increased in which epidemiological research results are submitted to courts to
settle causation conclusively. For example, they include the following: a lawsuit
raised by South Korean veterans of the Vietnam War and their families against the
Dow Chemical Co. in the USA claiming that a defoliant manufactured by this
company had been sprayed on the South Korean armed forces' operational areas
during the war and therefore led to the development of skin diseases among the
plaintiffs through exposure to the defoliant[9]; an air pollution lawsuit raised by the
residents of Seoul against the Republic of Korea (South Korean government), Seoul
Metropolitan Government, and automobile manufacturers[10]; a lawsuit raised by
smokers and their families against the state and tobacco companies[11]; and a lawsuit
raised by patients administered anti-hemophilia agents manufactured by Green
Cross Corp. demanding compensation from this company for damages, claiming
that the plaintiffs had been infected with the human immunodeficiency virus
(HIV).[12] Epidemiological research has thus been used to prove causation in diverse
lawsuits demanding compensation for damages including environmental pollution,
industrial disasters, and product liability.

These lawsuits have something in common: the victims' symptoms appeared
after considerable latent periods from exposure to particular risk factors, and factors
besides exposure to these risk factors, too, can lead to the development of the same
diseases. When the latent period is extensive, it becomes nearly impossible to
directly prove the association between exposure and a particular disease. However,
it is possible to measure the effects of exposure in the form of prevalence rates
within certain populations, and a junction between epidemiology and jurisprudence
can be created by estimating the causation between exposure and the incidence of
particular diseases based on these rates.[13]

When epidemiological research results are submitted as evidence, how their
proof value is to be judged by courts emerges as an important question in terms of
practical affairs. However, current examples of and precedents in practical affairs
are either unclear or inconsistent in their understanding of epidemiological causation. For example, in the air pollution lawsuit above, the judge first enumerated
diverse research results regarding epidemiological causation between air pollutants
such as fine dust and nitrogen dioxide and respiratory ailments and then denied such
epidemiological causation based on the reasons that research results acknowledging
correlation exhibited small relative risk (RR) and were inconsistent. On the other
hand, in the first instance of the tobacco lawsuit above, the judge acknowledged

---

[9]The Decision of the Appellate Court of Seoul 2002Na32686 (2006. 1. 26.)

[10]The Decision of the Appellate Court of Seoul 2010Na35659 (2010. 12. 23.)

[11]The Decision of the Appellate Court of Seoul 2007Na18883 (2011. 2. 15.)

[12]The Decision of the Supreme Court of Korea 2008Da16776 (2011. 9. 29.)

[13]The Decision of the Supreme Court of Korea 99Da41886 (1999. 12. 7.)

general causation between smoking and lung cancer based on epidemiological research results but ruled that specific causation between the plaintiffs' smoking and lung cancer had not been proven.[14] In contrast, in a review of the same lawsuit by an appellate court on an appeal, the judge ruled that specific causation could be estimated for cases, among these lung cancer patients, with a high association between the disease and smoking, or elderly males with a smoking history of 20 pack-years or above who had been diagnosed with squamous cell carcinoma or small-cell carcinoma.[15]

As discussed above, there is considerable confusion in practical affairs regarding how epidemiological research results are to be analyzed and evaluated in proving causation. Especially, noticeable are the absence of methodology in analyzing and evaluating epidemiological research and the confusion in legal principles concerning the question of estimating causation in individual cases based on epidemiological research results.

If observational association is genuine, is it causal? It shows two possible cases. First, exposure and disease are boxed, and there is causal association between exposure and disease indicated by the arrow. Second, although the same association between exposure and disease is observed as well, this is only because exposure and disease are each linked to a third factor, which is factor X. This association is the result of confounding and is not causal. There are considerable differences between clinical medicine and public health in distinguishing between confounding and causality. If the relationship is causal, it will be possible to successfully reduce the risk of coronary artery diseases by lowering the level of cholesterol in the blood. However, if the relationship stems from a confounder, a rise in the risk of coronary artery diseases is due to factor X so that lowering the level of cholesterol in the blood will have no effect on reducing the risk of coronary artery diseases. Consequently, it is necessary to distinguish between a causal association and a confounding association (i.e., non-causal).

In causal pathways, a particular factor acts as the cause of a particular disease without mediation in the case of direct causality. In contrast, in the case of indirect causality, a particular factor undergoes an intermediate mediation process and acts as the cause of a particular disease. Because causal mediators broadly biologically exist, epidemiological causation falls under any one of the four types below:

Necessary and sufficient relationship: In this type, a particular factor must be both necessary and sufficient for a particular disease to develop. The disease in question never develops without this particular factor and develops without fail if that factor does exist. However, such situations are rare even if they do occur.

Sufficient but unnecessary relationship: In this type, while particular factors can each cause a particular disease, there also exist other factors that act independently. In other words, exposure to either radiation or benzene causes leukemia even without any other factor. However, not everyone who has been exposed to either

---

[14]The Decision of the District Court of Seoul 99Gahap104973 (2007. 1. 25.)
[15]The Decision of the Appellate Court of Seoul 2007Na18883 (2011. 2. 15.)

radiation or benzene develops leukemia. Consequently, neither of the factors is necessary, and other supplementary factors exist as well.

Necessary but insufficient relationship: In this type, while all of the relevant factors are necessary, none of them alone is sufficient to cause the disease in question. Consequently, multiple factors that follow a particular temporal sequence are necessary. For example, the phenomenon of carcinogenesis undergoes a complex process that includes initiation and promotion. In other words, the activities first of the initiators and then of the promoters are both necessary for cancer to develop. Cancer does not develop with the activities of either the initiators or promoters alone.

Insufficient and unnecessary relationship: Finally, there are cases where a particular factor alone is neither sufficient nor necessary for the development of a particular disease. More complex, this type corresponds to causation that is applied to most chronic diseases.

Most chronic diseases develop not due to single factors alone but due to the negative effects of many factors on the human body over a long period of time. In addition, because epidemiological research examines populations, it makes use of figures concerning relative risk, odds ratios, and attributable risk levels as indices expressing associations between instances of exposure to harmful factors and the development of diseases through a range of data. For example, when the relative risk is 4.0, the danger of the development of a disease is four times as high for exposure groups as it is for non-exposure groups. Consequently, when used appropriately, such indices can serve as evidence for presuming a causal relation in court as well.

References

Battaglini, G. (1952). The exclusion of the concourse of causes in Italian Criminal Law. *Journal of Criminal Law, Criminology and Police Science, 43*, 441–450.

Black, B. (2000). A new metaphor for clarifying the difference between cause-in-fact and proximate cause. *Kansas Journal of Law & Public Policy, 10*, 159.

Calabresi, G. (1975). Concerning cause and the law of torts. *University of Chicago Law Review, 43*, 69–108.

Danermark, B., Ekstrom, M., Jakobsen, L., & Karlsson, J. (2005). *Explaining society: An introduction to critical realism in the social sciences*. New York, NY: Routledge.

Dix, G. (2009). *Gilbert Law summaries on criminal law* (18th ed.). London, UK: Gilbert.

Gotterbarn, D. (1971). Hume's two lights on cause. *Philosophical Quarterly, 21*, 168–171.

Hart, H. L. A., & Honoré, H. (1985). *Causation in the Law* (2nd ed.). Oxford: Clarendon.

Heathcote, A., & Armstrong, D. (1991). *Causes and Law* (p. 25). New York, NY: Nous.

Herring, J. (2010). *Criminal Law: Text, cases, and materials* (4th ed.). London, UK: Oxford University Press.

Hoeffe, O., & Ameriks, K. (2009). *Kant's Moral and legal philosophy*. London, UK: Cambridge University Press.

Honig, R. (1995). "Kausalität und objektive Zurechnung", Festgabe für Reinhard von Frank zum 70. Geburstag. In J. S. Lee et al. (Eds.), *Causation and objective imputation* (p. 1995). Pakyounsa: Seoul, Korea.

Hume, D. (1975). Enquiries concerning human understanding and concerning the principles of morals. In L. A. Selby-Bigge (Ed.), *An enquiry concerning the principles of morals* (3rd ed.). Oxford, UK: Oxford University Press.

Hume, D. (1978). A treatise of human nature. In L. A. Selby-Bigge (Ed.), *An enquiry concerning the principles of morals* (2nd ed.). Oxford, UK: Oxford University Press.

Imbens, G. W., & Rubin, D. B. (2015). *Causal inference for statistics, social, and biomedical sciences: An introduction.* London, UK: Cambridge University Press.

Jee, W. L. (2014). *Lecture on Civil Law* (12th ed.). Seoul: Hongmoonsa (In Korean).

Kaufmann, A. (1995a). "Kritisches zur Risikoerhöhurgstheorie" Festschrift für Hans-Heinrich Jescheck zum 70. Geburtstag, 1985. In J. S. Lee et al. (Eds.), *Theory of increasing risk and related issues.* Seoul, Korea: Pakyounsa.

Kaufman, A. (1995b). Objecktive Zurechnung beim Vorsatzdelkte" Festschrift für H. H. Jeschck, 1985. In J. S. Lee et al. (Eds.), *Objective imputation in intentional offense.* Seoul, Korea: Pakyounsa.

Kelley, P. J. (1991). Proximate cause in negligence law: history, theory, and the present darkness. *Washington University Law Review, 69*(1), 49–105.

Keyserlink, E. W. (1994). Assisted suicide, causality and the supreme court of Canada. *McGill Law Journal, 39*(3), 710–718.

Kim, S. Y. (2016). *Principles of Obligational Law.* Seoul, Korea: Hwasan Media (In Korean).

Koons, R. C. (2000). *Realism regained: An exact theory of causation, teleology, and the mind.* Oxford, UK: Oxford University Press.

LaFave, W. R. (2010). *Criminal Law* (5th ed.). New York, NY: West.

Lampe, E. (1995). "Die Kausalität und ihre strafrechtliche Fucktion" Armin Kaufmann Gedächtnissrift, 1989. In J. S. Lee et al. (Eds.), *Causation and its role in Criminal Law.* Seoul, Korea: Pakyounsa.

Lee, S. G. (2016). Proving causation with epidemiological evidence in tobacco lawsuits. *Journal of Preventive Medicine and Public Health, 49,* 80–96.

Lipton, P. (2004). *Evidence to the best explanation* (2nd ed.). New York, NY: Routledge.

Loux, M. (2006). *Metaphysics: A contemporary introduction* (3rd ed.). New York, NY: Tayor & Francis Group.

Malone, W. S. (1956). Ruminations on cause-in-fact. *Stanford Law Review, 9,* 60–99.

Millican, P. (2009). Hume, causal realism, and causal science. *Mind, 118*(471), 647–712.

Moore, M. S. (2009). *Causation and responsibility.* Oxford, UK: Oxford University Press.

Park, Y. H. (2002). Medical malpractice lawsuits and factual causation. *Journal of Justice, 45,* 284 (In Korean).

Robison, W. (1977). Hume's causal scepticism. In G. P. Morice (Ed.), *David Hume: Bicentenary papers* (pp. 156–166). Edinburgh, UK: Edinburgh University Press.

Robinson, J. A. (1962). Hume's two definition of cause. *Philosophical Quarterly, 12,* 162–171.

Robinson, P. H. (2008). *Criminal law-case studies & controversies* (2nd ed.). New York, NY: Wolters Kluwer.

Roxin, C. (1995). "Gedanken Zur Problematik der Zurechnung im Strafrecht" Festschrift für Richrard Honig, Göttingen, 1970. In J. S. Lee et al. (Eds.), *Reviews of objective imputation in Criminal Law* (pp. 48–49). Seoul, Korea: Pakyounsa.

Shin, E. J. (2012). Study of causation in medical malpractice cases. *Korean Journal of Medicine and Law, 20*(2), 191–217 (In Korean).

Smith, K. N. (1949). *The philosophy of David Hume: A critical study of its origin and central doctrines.* London, UK: Macmillan.

Spellman, B. A., & Kincannon, A. (2001). The relation between counterfactual ("But For") and causal reasoning: Experimental findings and implications for jurors' decisions. *Law and Contemporary Problems, 64,* 241–264.

Stapleton, J. (2001). Legal cause: Cause-in-fact and the scope of liability for consequences. *Vanderbilt Law Review, 54,* 941.

Strawson, G. (2014). *The secret connexion: Causation, realism, and David Hume.* Oxford, UK: Oxford University Press.

Stroud, B. (1978). Hume and the idea of causal necessity. *Philosophical Studies, 33,* 61–63.
Ulsenheimer, K. (1995). "Erfolgsrelevante und erfolgsneutrale Pflichtverletzungen im Rahmen der Fafhrlässigkeitsdelikte", Juristenzeitung, 1969. In J. S. Lee et al. (Eds.), *Results-related violation of duty and results-unrelated violation of duty in criminal negligence.* Seoul, Korea: Pakyounsa.
Watkins, E. (2005). *Kant and the metaphysics of causality.* Cambridge, UK: Cambridge University Press.
Worrall, J. L., & Moore, J. L. (2012). *Criminal Law.* New York, NY: Pearson.

Chapter 3
Methods in Epidemiology

Abstract Epidemiology is an academic discipline that determines the distribution of disease onsets and the causes of the development of diseases. However, when causal relations between individual victims' diseases and exposures are presumed based on prevalence rates among populations, a point of connection between epidemiology and jurisprudence is created. Epidemiology carefully examines whether observational associations among particular events are genuinely causal relations. For example, if the incidence rates of gastric cancer are very high among those who drink coffee frequently, coffee must be defined as a carcinogen. However, because the confounder of smoking mediates in this case and that it has generated gastric cancer, coffee is not the true cause. Consequently, epidemiology involves the collection of data through various experimental and observational studies to classify causal relations. For example, most chronic diseases develop not due to single factors alone but due to the negative effects of many factors on the human body over a long period of time. In addition, because epidemiological research examines populations, it makes use of figures concerning relative risk, odds ratios, and attributable risk levels as indices expressing associations between instances of exposure to harmful factors and the development of diseases through a range of data. For example, when the relative risk is 4.0, the danger of the development of a disease is four times as high for exposure groups as it is for non-exposure groups. Consequently, when used appropriately, such indices can serve as evidence for presuming a causal relation in court as well.

3.1 The Role of Epidemiology

Epidemiology is a public health methodology that studies the frequency and distribution of diseases that develop among populations and the factors that determine the distribution of such diseases (Gordis, 2013). The purpose of epidemiology intends to determine and prevent the cause of disease among populations.

© The Author(s), under exclusive licence to Springer Nature Singapore Pte Ltd., part of Springer Nature 2018
M. Jung, *An Investigation of the Causal Inference Between Epidemiology and Jurisprudence*,
SpringerBriefs in Philosophy, https://doi.org/10.1007/978-981-10-7862-0_3

Epidemiologists use statistical methods to verify and quantify the association between exposure to a particular risk factor, and this association may or may not be causal (Rothman, 2012: 1–7).

3.2 Epidemiological Investigation

3.2.1 Experimental Study and Observational Study

The ideal method to judge whether a factor is related to the aggravation of a disease or a symptom involves randomizing the subjects, dividing them into two groups, exposing only one of the two groups to a particular factor, and examine the members of each group after a certain duration so as to verify the cases of aggravation of a particular disease or symptom. Studies of this type are referred to as experimental studies or clinical trials (Black & Lilienfeld, 1984). Besides these studies, community trials, whose subjects represent all local communities instead of individual patients, are another experimental method of epidemiology.

In community trials, two similar local communities are selected to measure the incidence or prevalence rate of a particular disease that is to be studied or the level of risk factors for which an intervention is to be implemented. Once an intervention, including the intake of a substance with protective effects, such as fluorine has been implemented with only one of these local communities, differences in the levels of incidence of the relevant disease or degree of harm in the two areas after a certain duration of time are compared and interpreted as a result with respect to the presence or absence of the intervention (Ahn et al., 2005: 280). While this method is advantageous as the researcher can control the research environment, experimental studies have a disadvantage as they can be used only when evaluating the value of the factors that are considered helpful to people (e.g., new drugs or new treatments). This is because it is ethically impermissible to expose people consciously to factors known to be harmful.

On the other hand, the method in which people who have already been exposed to a harmful factor is observed and the results are compared to those who have not been exposed to the factor is called an observational study. Unlike experimental studies, in which risk factors are controlled and randomized participants are selected, observational studies have the potential for producing distorted research results due to other risk factors existing other than exposure to the particular harmful factor.

3.2.2 Types of Observational Study

Observational studies encompass diverse research methods including cross-sectional studies, ecological studies, cohort studies, and case–control studies. Among them, the most frequently used are cohort studies and case–control studies.

Cohort study: Cohort studies constitute a type of research in which the groups to be studied are classified according to their respective exposure to a factor causing disease, and each group is observed for a certain duration of time in order to verify the incidence of a particular disease. Cohort studies are classified into prospective cohort studies and retrospective cohort studies according to the methods that the researcher uses to collect data on exposure factors and the incidence of the disease. Prospective cohort studies constitute a method for which data on exposure factors are collected at the initial stages of the research, and then data on the incidence of the disease from that moment to a certain time point in the future are collected. Retrospective cohort studies constitute a method in which data on exposure factors at a certain time point in the past are collected and then data on the incidence of the disease from that moment to the present moment are collected. In any case, the researcher classifies the groups that are to be studied according to their respective exposure to the factor and then compares the incidence rates of the disease to the exposure group and non-exposure group, determining a correlation based on the derived figures. This is expressed diagrammatically as in the table below. By comparing in the table the non-exposure group's disease incidence rate, or $c/(a + c)$, and the exposure group's disease incidence rate, or $d/(b + d)$, the researcher can evaluate that the greater the differences are, the stronger the causal relationship is:

	Disease group	Healthy group	Sum	Ratios of disease onset
Non-exposed	a	c	$a + c$	$c/(a + c)$
Exposed	b	d	$b + d$	$d/(b + d)$

Cohort studies are advantageous in that the temporal relationship between exposure and a disease is more easily proven than through other research methods. However, they have limitation as elements other than exposure to a factor can give rise to biases in the research results and that when the incidence rate of the disease being studied is low, participants at a large scale need to be observed for a considerable duration of time (Greenberg et al., 2005: 132–146). Although retrospective cohort studies do not require long-term observation because the disease has already developed, verifying the incidence of the disease depends on such records, so potential for errors when inferring the results increases when records are either absent or inaccurate.

Case–control studies: Case–control studies constitute a method in which a group with a particular disease (the case group) and a group without a particular disease (the control group) are selected, and the degree of the respective exposure to a particular factor between the both groups is compared. When there is a correlation between the exposure and a disease, the exposure rate in the case group is higher than that in the control group. Case–control studies are useful to investigate diseases with comparatively low incidence rates or long latency periods, such as cancer. Although time is needed to allow for the incidence of an adequate number of cases or large-scale case groups must be secured for cohort studies, case–control studies do not entail such requirements (Greenberg et al., 2005: 147–161).

3.3   Interpretations of Epidemiological Results

To prove the existence of a causal relationship between exposure to a risk factor and disease, an association between such an exposure and the disease must be first proven. Nevertheless, the existence of an association does not necessarily mean there is an existence of a causal relationship. However, when the degree of association is strong, it becomes easier to judge that a causal relationship exists. Scholars express the degree of association as a relative risk (RR), odds ratio (OR), and attributable risk (AR), all of which are numerical expressions of the degree of risk of the incidence of a disease after exposure to a risk factor (Ahn et al., 2005: 73).

3.3.1   Relative Risk

RR is defined as the ratio of the incidence rate of a disease among people that are not exposed to a risk to that among people exposed to the risk (Gordis, 2013: 243–261). Here, the incidence rate of a disease is the value obtained by dividing the number of patients who have developed a disease in a particular group over a certain duration of time by the total number of the group's members. In contrast, the figure representing people with a particular disease in the group that is studied referred to as the prevalence rate. For example, let us suppose that research is conducted on a group consisting of 200 people exposed to a risk factor and another group consisting of 400 people unexposed to the factor. When the number of people diagnosed have a particular disease in the exposure group and in the non-exposure group after one year amounts to 50 and 10, respectively, the incidence rate in the exposure group is 0.25 (=50/200) and the incidence rate in the non-exposure group is 0.025 (=10/400), which yields a RR of 10.0 (=0.25/0.025). When the RR is 10.0, this indicates that the risk of the incidence of the disease in the exposure group is ten times greater than that in the non-exposure group. On the other hand, when the RR is 1.0, the risk in the exposure group and the risk in the non-exposure group are identical, which indicates that there is no association between exposure to a risk factor and the disease (Rothman, 2012: 38–68). However, when the RR is greater than 1.0, a positive association exists between exposure to the risk factor and the disease, and a causal relationship may be acknowledged. In contrast, when the RR is smaller than 1.0, exposure to the risk factor reduces the risk of the incidence of the disease, which can be interpreted to indicate that the exposure to the factor has an effect of preventing disease.

3.3.2 Odds Ratio

OR is mainly used to indicate an association between exposure to the factor and the disease in case–control studies (Gordis, 2013: 215–229; Rothman, 2012: 38–68). OR is defined as the ratio of odds of the exposure to the factor in the case group to that in the control group. Odds are the ratio of the likelihood of the occurrence of two mutually exclusive events. For example, the likelihood of winning for two players A and B in a sports game can be expressed as the ratio of the number of people who have predicted A's victory to the number of people who have predicted B's victory. When the number of people who has predicted A's victory amounts to 30 and the number of people who have predicted B's victory amounts to 40, respectively, the odds are expressed as 30/40. The higher the likelihood of A's victory and the lower the likelihood of B's victory, the higher the value of the odds estimated. When explained in a table format, it appears as follows. Here, OR is the value obtained by dividing the exposure odds of the case group by those of the control group:

	Patient group	Control group
Exposed	a	b
Non-exposed	c	d

In addition, the OR according to the table presented above is expressed as follows. Let us suppose that in a case–control study including a case group consisting of 50 people and a control group consisting of 50 people, 30 people and 10 people in the case and control groups are confirmed to have been exposed to a risk factor, respectively. Here, OR = (30/20)/(10/40) = 6.0:

$$OR = \frac{(a/c)}{(b/d)}$$

If the disease under question is rare, the OR will approximate the RR. Consequently, it is possible to judge, through the OR, that the risk of developing the disease under question is six times greater among people who have been exposed to the risk factor. In other words, the OR is used to estimate the RR with figures obtained from case–control studies when the disease under question is so rare that cohort studies cannot be conducted.

3.3.3   Attributable Risk

AR refers to the ratio at which a risk factor is statistically attributable to a disease. The goal of all observational studies is to judge the relative risk of the incidence of a disease in association with exposure to a particular factor. However, the RR only indicates the degree of an association. Thus, the AR statistically expresses the association between a certain factor and a disease in a population (Gordis, 2013: 215–229; Rothman, 2012: 38–68). This is also called the "attributable fraction." On the other hand, the aspect of a particular disease among the entire population that has been judged to have occurred due to the activation of a particular factor is called the general population AR (i.e., PAR) and it is classified separately.

Originally, to express the maximum aspect of a particular disease that can be attributed to exposure to a particular risk factor, AR can be prevented by eliminating this exposure or blocking its effect. For example, if lung cancer is attributable to smoking from among the risk factors of the disease in a certain nation, the incidence rate of lung cancer will decrease by 70% in that country when smoking is prohibited. Here, the AR is expressed as follows:

$$AR = \frac{(\text{Ratios of disease onset among exposed group}) - (\text{Ratios of disease onset among non-exposed group})}{\text{Ratios of disease onset among exposed group}}.$$

$$= \frac{I_1 - I_0}{I_1} = 1 - \frac{1}{RR} = \frac{RR - 1}{RR}$$

For example, let us suppose that research on 100 people who are exposed to a particular risk factor and 300 who are people unexposed to a particular risk factor has been initiated and that a particular disease has developed among 70 people in the exposure group and among 30 people in the non-exposure group, respectively, after one year. Here, because the disease has developed in 70 out of 100 people in the exposure group and in 30 people out of 300 people (i.e., 10 out of 100) in the non-exposure group, respectively, the incidence of the disease among 60 out of 70 people (i.e., 85%) in the exposure group is considered attributable to exposure to this risk factor. As shown in the equation above, the AR can be calculated when the RR is known. For the AR to amount to 100%, the RR must be unlimited. This indicates that the particular factor is the only cause behind the incidence of the disease. Taking note of this point, when the RR reaches a certain level or higher, causal relationships can be acknowledged in individual and specific cases (Green, 1992).

3.4   Causal Misinterpretations in Epidemiology

As with the results of all scientific studies, fallacies occur in epidemiological analyses as well. The relative risk may be greater than 1 even when there is no actual association, and vice versa. In general, errors are caused by chance, biases, and confounders (Gordis, 2013: 262–278; Rothman, 2012: 124–147). In particular, epidemiologists classify errors into random errors and systematic errors and call the latter biases. While random errors decrease when the number of study subjects is increased, the same does not hold true for systematic errors. On the other hand, confounding, unlike biases, occurs when there exist an observational association between a confounder and a disease. When the results of epidemiological studies are submitted to lawsuits as evidence, judges have the responsibility to distinguish between fallacies and real causation in epidemiological associations. The types and significance of epidemiological fallacies are examined below:

Chance: When a coin is tossed and yields heads (face-up side) on all ten occasions, this is called the result of chance. Chance can act on epidemiological studies as well. For example, while there may be no association between electromagnetic waves and stomach cancer, a relative risk greater than 1 can be yielded by chance. Such a possibility of observing an association due to chance is indicated with the p value in statistics (Rothman, 2012: 124–147). If the p value is 0.2, this means that even though there is no actual association, the possibility for the production of such a relative risk due to chance amounts to 20%. To reduce fallacies due to chance, epidemiologists think that the p value must remain below a certain level for research results to be statistically significant (Egilman, Kim, & Biklen 2003). This is called the alpha value (a value) or the significance level. Here, the p value is unrelated to the degree of proof demanded in civil suits (Kaye, 1987). However, the smaller the p value is, the smaller the possibility of errors is due to chance. Consequently, some believe that the p value must be 0.01 or below for the results of epidemiological studies to be used as evidence for acknowledging legal causation.

Some researchers prefer the confidence interval to the p value as an index for evaluating an observational association in epidemiological studies (Cohen, 1985). This means that the figures derived from a study are interval estimates instead of point estimates. For example, when the confidence interval amounts to 95%, this means that when new samples are extracted from the same group and yield repetitive results, 95% of the results are predicted to fall within that interval. Although it shows the scope of the relative risk, the confidence interval is no proof positive that actual risk will exist within that interval, just as the p value is not a figure guaranteeing the accuracy of research results. It is only that the broader the confidence interval is, the greater the possibility of errors is due to chance and that the narrower the confidence interval is, the smaller such a possibility is (Gordis, 2013: 262–278; Rothman, 2012: 124–147).

Biases: Causal fallacies, the second type, are called systematic errors or biases. Mainly problematic are selection biases, or biases in the process of selecting research data, and information biases, or biases in the process of classifying research data.

First, selection biases are errors arising from the ways study subjects are selected. For example, research results can be distorted when study subjects are selected as the control group for a study because they have been exposed to a factor hypothesized to have an association with the disease in question. For instance, in selecting the control group to study the association between smoking and heart diseases if volunteers are included in the control group because of their family history of heart diseases as smokers, the association between smoking and heart diseases may turn out to be higher than it actually is due to genetic factors. On the other hand, in a patient control group study on the association between smoking and lung cancer, if the control group is selected from among patients who have been hospitalized for diseases that are considered unrelated to smoking, research results can be distorted when the smoking rate of the control group is higher than that of the public. In addition, in a cohort study on an exposure group consisting of factory workers and a non-exposure group consisting of members of the public other than factory workers, selection biases can arise if the non-exposure group includes people who cannot work due to poor health. This is called the "healthy worker effect" (Ahn et al., 2005: 307–330). Nevertheless, the existence of a selection bias does not make the results of a study useless. When the relative risk is high, the effect of selection bias can be seen as limited. In addition, when a similar degree of association is observed among diverse control groups, the validity of the results can be seen as unaffected even when a selection bias exists in any one of these control groups. In addition, even when a dose–response relationship, which will be examined later, is consistently observed in various groups with disparate exposure doses, a selection bias in a particular exposure group can be said to affect the overall results only slightly (Gordis, 2013: 262–278).

Second, information biases refer to the occurrence of errors in research results due to the collection of inaccurate information in the process of gathering information on study subjects' past exposure to a risk factor through surveys or interviews. Because the researcher cannot but rely on information on past facts to determine the exposure, disease, and temporal relationship between the two in studies with patient control groups, information biases become important problems. When the researcher interviews study subjects and seeks to obtain information on the pathways, duration, and degree of exposure while relying on the subjects' memory, the results can be distorted because, in general, people with diseases strive more than those without diseases to retrieve memories of exposure (Rothman, 2012: 124–147; Greenberg et al., 2005). If information on exposure or the state of a disease can be collected from objective and reliable data, information biases can be reduced. On the other hand, the accuracy of interview results is determined by whether the study subjects are reliable and whether the same contents can be verified through other data. Inaccurate diagnoses of the state of a disease, too, can give rise to information biases. Consequently, to judge the validity of the results of an epidemiological study, one must also verify whether the methods for diagnosing diseases were appropriate and precise. Diseases must be acknowledged and clearly defined to make accurate diagnoses possible. In addition, diagnoses must comply with the standards generally approved in medical circles.

Confounders: Confounding occurs when there is another causal element that confounds the relationship between risk factors and the results. For example, even though the results of research on the association between asbestos and lung cancer show the existence of an association, when the smoking rate of workers who treat asbestos is higher than that of the general population, a causal relationship between asbestos and lung cancer cannot be asserted conclusively based on the same results (Gordis, 2013: 262–278). This is because smoking may have acted together in the development of lung cancer. Such confounding can occur in observational studies because study subjects are not assigned to the comparative group in a randomized manner, unlike in experimental studies. When a confounder has been verified, researchers take this into consideration and design studies with methods such as matching and stratification. If an association between risk exposure and a disease emerges even after adjustments have been made regarding the confounder, its causal association is then determined.

References

Ahn, Y. O., Yoo, G. Y., Park, B. J., Kim, D. H., Bae, J. M., Khang, D. H., et al. (2005). *Epidemiology: The principles and applications*. Gwanak-gu: Seoul National University Press. (In Korean).

Black, B., & Lilienfeld, D. E. (1984). Epidemiologic proof in toxic tort litigation. *Fordham Law Review, 52*(5), 732–785.

Cohen, N. B. (1985). Confidence in probability: Burdens of persuasion in a world of imperfect knowledge. *New York University Law Review, 60,* 385.

Egilman, D., Kim, J., & Biklen, M. (2003). Proving causation: The use and abuse of medical and scientific evidence inside the courtroom—An epidemiologist's critique of the judicial interpretation of the Daubert ruling. *Food and Drug Law Journal, 58*(2), 223–250.

Gordis, L. (2013). *Epidemiology* (5th ed.). London, UK: Saunders.

Green, M. D. (1992). Expert witnesses and sufficiency of evidence in toxic substances litigation: The legacy of agent orange and bendectin litigation. *Northwestern University Law Review, 86* (3), 643–699.

Greenberg, R. S., Daniels, S. R., Flanders, W. D., Eley, J. W., & Boring, J. R. (2005). *Medical epidemiology* (4th ed.). London, UK: McGraw-Hill.

Kaye, D. H. (1987). Apples and oranges: Confidence coefficients and the burden of persuasion. *Cornell Law Review, 73*(1), 4–77.

Rothman, K. J. (2012). *Epidemiology: An introduction* (2nd ed.). Oxford, UK: Oxford University Press.

Chapter 4
Debates on Causation in Tobacco Lawsuits

Abstract With regard to smoking-related lawsuits today, the grounds on which plaintiffs arguing damages due to smoking charge criminal defendants with legal responsibility have developed from the existing responsibility for illegal harmful acts into struggles over a new legal principle since the legislation of the South Korean Product Liability Act. According to this legal principle, tobacco is a defective product, and criminal defendants can be charged with legal responsibility when plaintiffs suffer damages due to tobacco and prove the probability of the occurrence of damage regarding a causal relation between the defects of tobacco and the occurrence of the damage. However, lung cancer, which is a chronic disease, develops only after long-term exposure to smoking and can involve interventions of other factors as well, which complicates the determination of causal relations. Consequently, as in the medical malpractice lawsuits examined above, mitigation of the plaintiffs' burden of proof can be considered. However, the South Korean Supreme Court, which has ruled in favor of criminal defendants in smoking-related lawsuits filed by the plaintiffs, has not sufficiently accepted epidemiological evidence in proving causal relations. The reasoning is that even when epidemiological correlations are acknowledged in the case of non-specific diseases such as lung cancer, the plaintiffs must prove aspects including the exposure time regarding harmful factors, the degree of their exposures to these factors, the time of disease onset, health status before exposure to the harmful factors, and lifestyles and must thus prove the probability of the causation of non-specific diseases by those factors. In other words, the South Korean Supreme Court has judged that epidemiological evidence fails to be valuable evidence in lawsuits to determine responsibility for the occurrence of damage to individuals because epidemiological research studies populations instead of individuals. Moreover, while negligence can be seen as existing when tobacco companies, manufacturers of harmful products, have failed sufficiently to notify consumers of the harms of tobacco, the Supreme Court has ruled that these companies have appropriately performed their duty of describing potential risks, which in this case consists of what are known as the instruction defects of products.

M. Jung, *An Investigation of the Causal Inference Between Epidemiology and Jurisprudence*, SpringerBriefs in Philosophy, https://doi.org/10.1007/978-981-10-7862-0_4

55

4.1 Legal Perspectives

Epidemiological studies showing that the risk of developing lung cancer is sig-
nificantly higher for smokers than it is for non-smokers have been consistently
presented since the 1950s (Doll & Hill, 1954; Hill, Millar, & Connelly, 2003).
Consequently, smokers who think that they have developed lung cancer due to
smoking have raised lawsuits against cigarette firms, demanding compensation for
damages (Rutter, 1997). In the case of tobacco lawsuits, the grounds on which
plaintiffs claiming damages have held defendants legally responsible have tended to
develop from general unlawful conduct to new arguments in legal principles since
the legislation of the Product Liability Act. According to these legal principles,
tobacco is a product with defects, and plaintiffs have been subjected to damages due
to it. Therefore, it is possible to hold defendants legally responsible if plaintiffs can
prove the probability of damage occurrence regarding the causal relationship
between the defects of tobacco and damage occurrence. This is because unless
cigarette firms, which are the defendants, present evidence that they have no
involuntary fault, their involuntary fault can be presumed if plaintiffs prove that
damages have occurred due to the defects of tobacco. In the Product Liability Act,
the defects of a product refer to a state in which that product lacks the safety
commonly expected of it, considering the characteristics and commonly predicted
form of use of the product, the period in which the manufacturer distributed the
product, and other conditions related to the product. Consequently, while lawsuits
seeking compensation for damages due to products with defects can be classified as
those involving product liabilities, it is questionable whether the probability theory
on causal relationships or the de facto presumption of involuntary fault in the
arguments above constitutes a judicial precedent generally acknowledged in product liability lawsuits.

Plaintiffs argue that because the defects of a product concern the safety linked to
the risks of damages that the components of the product will incur to life and body,
if tobacco causes in smokers diverse diseases including lung cancer in the long term
and makes smoking cessation difficult due to its addictiveness, it either is a product
with defects or has such design defects. In addition, the manufacturers' duty to
remove risks is imposed broadly from manufacturers to distributors. Thus, this
consists of more than simply informing consumers of the risks. In other words, this
includes the duty to actively publicize the risks so that consumers may become
adequately aware of them (Lee, 2016). According to this viewpoint, it becomes
difficult for cigarette firms to be free from the responsibility of stating their product
"warning defects" if they have not fully performed the duty.

When the product's "design defects" are first examined, it is difficult to argue
that tobacco sold in the market has failed to reach the levels of safety commonly
expected by members of the public. The notable exceptions in these circumstances
are the insertion of special substances in tobacco by defendants to strengthen the
product's addictiveness. Manufacturing defects refer to situations in which a product becomes dangerous because it has been manufactured and processed

differently from its originally intended design despite the manufacturer's performance of its duty of care regarding the manufacture and processing of that product (Lee, 2016). Consequently, it is difficult legally to acknowledge the design defects of tobacco based on this product's health risks and addictiveness. "Warning defects" occur when a manufacturer has not faithfully performed its duty of explaining to consumers the risks of a product. In the risk society of today, a manufacturer has a duty to inform and warn consumers about a product so that the latter may independently and rationally adjust the specific risks of that product and protect themselves. Considering factors including the addictiveness of tobacco and the effect of smoking on adolescents, it is difficult to say that warning messages on tobacco products distributed in the market such as "Smoking causes diverse diseases including lung cancer and will render even my family and neighbors ill" and "Cigarette smoke contains 2-naphthylamine, nickel, benzene, vinyl chloride, arsenic, and cadmium, which are carcinogenic substances" have an adequate warning effect. There also exist pictorial warning labels which are more active measures. However, there is much room for legal argument regarding whether such warning defects have directly caused the development of lung cancer or negative health outcomes in plaintiffs and how much involuntary fault can be ascribed to defendants with respect to such damages.

In judging legal responsibilities for the two types of defects examined above, the question of causal relationships arises. It is possible to calculate the probability of developing lung cancer and the contribution of smoking under specific conditions as statistical figures by considering the characteristics of the injured party such as the duration of smoking, the amount of tobacco smoked, and the age of smoking initiation in epidemiological data. Consequently, plaintiffs argue that when smokers develop lung cancer, it is possible to make de facto presumptions regarding whether smoking has caused the cancer based on objective data. In addition, cigarette firms, as the defendants, have a responsibility to disprove that the plaintiffs' lung cancer has not been caused by smoking. In principle, when specific damages have been incurred by the defects of a product, the burden of proof regarding that product's design defects or warning defects lies with the plaintiffs, who are the injured party. However, when the causal relationship between specific risk factors and the development of diseases has been proven scientifically and solidly, the burden of proof on the injured party, the plaintiffs, may be reduced. This is because when a product is an aggregation of state-of-the-art technology or it is extremely difficult for members of the public other than experts to detect defects in product liability lawsuits, causal relationships may be presumed for the fair burdening of damages. For example, the trend today is partly to reduce the burden of proof even in judicial precedents regarding pollution lawsuits or medical malpractice lawsuits because demanding strict proof for causal relationships can result in injustice to plaintiffs.

Another point of contention that must be heeded in tobacco lawsuits is defendants' intent and negligence. Injured patients argue for the existence of involuntary fault in which cigarette firms, as manufacturers of a harmful product, have failed to inform consumers of important information on the product, which should have been publicized and should have been fulfilled to protect consumers' bodies and lives.

This is because involuntary fault is presumed when damage to consumers has been proven in a situation where a product has defects. Moreover, for injured patients, the plaintiffs argue that intentionality can be acknowledged because cigarette firms have concealed information on tobacco's addictiveness and harmfulness while promoting the sales of tobacco by encouraging smoking, improving the taste and aroma of diverse cigarette brands, or increasing the nicotine absorption rate instead. However, because it is difficult actually to prove intentionality, the question of the de facto presumption of involuntary fault is a point of contention in tobacco lawsuits.

In general, the party being accused of involuntary fault should have been aware of the occurrence of particular results but has failed to recognize the risks due to its carelessness. In other words, involuntary fault in tobacco lawsuits consists of a state of deliberation in which cigarette firms, the defendants, have manufactured tobacco carelessly even though they should have been aware of the possibility of the development of lung cancer in consumers. The problem is that the burden of proof regarding whether defendants have committed involuntary fault lies with the plaintiffs. Courts' normative judgment is that defendants have not committed involuntary fault if and when cigarette firms argue that they too have been aware only of the general predictability of the development of cancer with respect to the risks of tobacco. However, because it is difficult to directly prove involuntary fault that is merely under deliberation, when special circumstances or particular circumstantial evidence is judged to exist, it is also possible to presume the involuntary fault of the injured party from such circumstantial evidence (in accordance with empirical rules). In addition, the duty to warn about the risks of tobacco can be applied more strictly to the case of minors because they possess less ability to make judgments than that of adults. However, the manufacturers' responsibility for compensation for damages is reduced through comparative negligence in cases where plaintiffs have voluntarily smoked despite the risks because the fault lies with them as well.

4.2 Epidemiological Perspectives

In general, the relative risk of lung cancer occurrence is over 20 times higher for smokers than it is for lifelong non-smokers (Wu-Williams & Samet, 2000). However, tobacco firms argue that because epidemiological evidence for the causality between smoking and lung cancer occurrence is merely a statistical association concerning populations, it cannot serve as evidence for the cause of the outbreak in individual lung cancer patients. In other words, they contend that long-term smoking does not lead to the occurrence of lung cancer in all smokers and that not all lung cancer patients have engaged in smoking. Of course, lung cancer occurrence is related also to factors including outdoor and indoor air pollution, occupational exposure to harmful materials, drinking, and alimentary (dietary) habits. Consequently, defendants, or tobacco firms, argue that plaintiffs must prove the high probability that specific individuals would not have developed lung cancer if they had not smoked. To make causal judgments on the causes of a disease, the relationship between the explanatory power of a specific risk factor and inter-individual variations in disease occurrence must be examined. At the same time, this must not be confounded with the magnitude of a causal contribution of a specific risk factor to disease occurrence (Davey Smith, 2011). In relation to the causality between smoking and lung cancer, inter-individual variations in disease occurrence can be expressed as follows: Lung cancer patients include non-smokers as well, and only one out of ten smokers develops lung cancer. These points are important to tobacco firms hoping to refute the causal association between smoking and lung cancer on individual levels.

Inter-individual variations in disease occurrence are explained by heritable factors, shared environmental factors, and non-shared environmental factors (Lichtenstein et al., 2000). These factors are separate from indices for evaluating the causal contribution of specific factors to disease occurrence such as the attributable fraction and the population attributable fraction. If and when heritable factors explain the bulk of inter-individual variations, they are classified as hereditary disorders. However, this does not mean that environmental factors are not involved in the occurrence of hereditary disorders. The proportion to which heritable factors explain inter-individual variations in phenotypes is called heritability, and this is because heritable factors do not signify the power of causal influence over disease occurrence (Burton, Tobin, & Hopper, 2005). Shared environmental factors can be found in twins who have been raised in the same home and have been exposed to passive (secondhand) smoking or have similar alimentary habits (Lichtenstein et al., 2000). The power to which an environmental factor not shared by twins explains inter-individual variations in disease occurrence is called the explanatory power of a non-shared environmental factor. Accordingly, previous studies have elucidated the degree to which heritable factors, shared environmental factors, and non-shared environmental factors explain inter-individual variations in the occurrence of cancer. Non-shared environmental factors exhibit the greatest influence when explaining inter-individual variations (Lichtenstein et al., 2000; Plomin, 2011). On the other hand, the power of smoking to explain inter-individual variations in lung cancer has been reported at approximately 10% (Pearce, 2011). This is a relatively high figure in comparison with those for other risk factors.

In tobacco lawsuits, lung cancer is considered not as a "specific disease," for which the causes and the results clearly correspond to each other, but as a "non-specific disease," for which diverse causative factors act together to develop the disease. Because the probability of not developing lung cancer is higher than that of developing the disease even when a smoker continues to smoke throughout his or her life (Peto et al., 2000), the risks and causal relationship of smoking leading to the outbreak of a specific disease in a specific individual is unclear. Consequently, tobacco firms argue that there is no 1:1 association between smoking and lung cancer because the logical statement, "B does not exist without A," applies to the relationship between the two. However, an association in which the causes and the results clearly correspond to each other is an 1:1 association, or monocause (A), that satisfies the necessary and sufficient conditions for the development of disease (B), cannot exist (Broadbent, 2013: 26–55). A classification of diseases themselves into specific diseases and non-specific diseases is not easily acceptable to epidemiologists.

While infectious diseases may be seen as "specific diseases" according to traditional definitions, this is not always the case. Although a large number of the South Korean population carries the tuberculous bacillus (*Mycobacterium tuberculosis*), the proportion of tuberculosis patients in the total population is very small (Hong, Kim, Lew, Lee, & Han, 1998). The cholera bacterium (*Vibrio cholerae*) and the tuberculous bacillus are necessary conditions for the development of cholera and tuberculosis, respectively. In other words, the attributable fraction is 100% for both the cholera germ and the tuberculous bacillus. One will not develop cholera unless one has been infected with the cholera germ, and one will not develop tuberculosis unless one has been infected with the tuberculous bacillus. However, with the exception of infectious diseases, most non-infectious diseases do not have necessary conditions. This is because risk factors are component causes in non-infectious diseases (Rothman, Greenland, & Lash, 2008). If specificity signifies the magnitude of the causal relationship between risk factors and diseases, as with the cholera bacterium and cholera, and tuberculous bacillus and tuberculosis, smoking, whose attributable fraction with respect to lung cancer amounts to 90%, can be seen as a very "specific" factor from among many other risk factors. In particular, of the primary types of lung cancer (small-cell lung cancer, squamous cell lung cancer, and laryngeal cancer) stated in tobacco lawsuits today, squamous cell lung cancer exhibits a considerable magnitude of specificity.

Epidemiology has played a significant role in proving the causal association between smoking and lung cancer and quantifying the degree of risk of smoking. However, the results of observations such as individual observations, animal experiments, and experimental analysis of chemical agents have contributed considerably to the formation of the grounds for the causal association between smoking and lung cancer (Proctor, 2012). Representatives are the results of the "tobacco juice" animal experiments, which showed the development of tumors by applying the tar in cigarettes to the backs of mice (Wynder, Graham, & Croninger, 1953). The results of chemical analyses of carcinogenic substances in tobacco smoke such as polycyclic aromatic hydrocarbons (PAHs) also helped to prove the causality between smoking and lung cancer (Proctor, 2012).

4.3   Tobacco Lawsuit Cases in Korea

The Korean National Health Insurance (NHI) system is operated by the National Health Insurance Service (NHIS) under the supervision of the government and provides health security based on Bismarckian social insurance principles (Lee, Chun, Lee, & Seo, 2008; Kim, 2010). NHI in Korea is compulsory and is a universal social insurance program that covers the entire population. The single insurer, the NHIS, has improved the equity of insurance contributions and the efficiency of managerial operations by converting a society-based corporatist system with multiple insurers into a unified managed system (Kim & Lee, 2010). South Korean men's smoking rates are high among member states of the Organization for Economic Cooperation and Development (OECD), and the ensuing cancer incidence rates and cancer mortality rates are considerable as well (Park, Jee, Shin, & Park, 2014). In addition, the national healthcare expenses used to treat various diseases caused by smoking, too, are on an immense scale. To suppress all of this, several cancer patients filed a lawsuit against tobacco companies both at home and at abroad, claiming compensation for damages based on a causal relationship between smoking and lung cancer emergence, but was rejected by the Supreme Court of South Korea.[1] When diagnosed with non-small-cell lung carcinomata and bronchioloalveolar carcinomata, which are types of lung cancer, A, with a smoking history of 30 or more pack years, and B, with a smoking history of 40 or more pack years, filed the present case against parties manufacturing and selling tobacco including the state, claiming compensation for damages. The Supreme Court ruled that the original judgment, which had not acknowledged a causal relationship between A's and B's smoking and their development of lung cancer, was justified. When examined more closely, the main points of the Supreme Court precedent are as follow.

Generally, those who make and sell products must manufacture products having safety within an expectable range in their structures, quality, and performance in reflection of current technological levels and economic feasibility and become liable for compensation due to illegal acts if and when damages arise to users due to defects in products stemming from the failure to secure such safety. From among such defects, important are the so-called design defects, which mainly consist of cases where products fail to be safe because manufacturers have not adopted reasonable alternative designs and therefore have failed to reduce or avoid damages and risks. Consequently, the South Korean Supreme Court has judged whether products have design defects both in consideration of diverse aspects including the characteristics and usages of products, contents of users' expectations of products, contents of expected risks, users' perception of risks, possibility of risk aversion by users, possibility and economic costs of alternative designs, and relative advantages and disadvantages of adopted designs and alternative designs and in reflection of socially accepted ideas.

In the present case, where the presence or absence of design defects in tobacco manufactured by parties including the state became the issue, the South Korean Supreme Court ruled that even if there were methods by which parties including the state could eliminate nicotine or tar completely, these parties' failure to adopt such methods could not in themselves be seen as design defects in reflection of points including the following: Burning strip-leaves and inhaling the smoke were the essential characteristics of tobacco use; the flavor of tobacco changed according to

---

[1]The Decision of the Supreme Court of Korea 2011Da22092 (2014. 4. 10.).

the amounts of nicotine and tar; tobacco consumers selected and smoked tobacco products that had flavors or aromas to their liking; and tobacco consumers smoked with the intention of obtaining the medicinal effects of nicotine such as a sense of stability or security. In addition, the Court upheld the original judgment, which had not found design defects in tobacco, because there was no evidence to acknowledge that tobacco companies had possessed but had not adopted reasonable alternative designs capable of reducing damages or risks to tobacco consumers due to smoking.

Of course, the South Korean Supreme Court acknowledged responsibility due to illegal acts regarding warning defects, where parties including manufacturers could have attached but had violated reasonable explanations, instructions, or warnings, thus reducing or avoiding the possible emergence of damages or risks due to the products in question (Lee, 2016). However, the Court ruled that when the presence or absence of such defects was judged, diverse aspects including products' characteristics, forms in which products are customarily used, contents of users' expectations of products, contents of expected risks, users' awareness of risks, and possibility of risk aversion by users must be comprehensively taken into consideration.

In the present case, where the presence or absence of warning defects in tobacco manufactured and sold by the state became the issue, it is a well-known fact that, through media reports and mandatory (legal) control, the possibility for smoking to cause cancer and diverse diseases in the lungs and respiratory organs is broadly recognized throughout society. However, the South Korean Supreme Court judged not only that the continuation and initiation of smoking were issues of choice according to free will but also that tobacco consumers widely recognized the possible difficulty of ceasing smoking once the habit had been initiated. Consequently, the Court supported the original judgment, according to which it was difficult to see tobacco as having warning defects just because parties including the state, tobacco manufacturers, had not attached additional explanations or warnings besides attaching cigarette warning labels in accordance with legal regulations.

When diagnosed with lung cancer after having smoking for a long time, A and B filed the present case against parties that manufactured and sold tobacco including the state, claiming compensation for damages. The South Korean Supreme Court ruled in the present case that a causal relationship could not be acknowledged between A's and B's smoking and their development of lung cancer. As the reasons, the Supreme Court cited grounds, such as lung cancer was not a specific disease caused solely by smoking but was a non-specific disease that could emerge through the complex interactions of external environmental factors including physical, biological, and chemical factors and biomechanical factors; non-small-cell lung carcinomata also included types of lung cancer that had no or very little association with smoking; and bronchioloalveolar carcinomata, a kind of adenocarcinomata, had a very low association with smoking in comparison with squamous cell carcinomata and small-cell lung carcinomata and had high incidence rates even among non-smokers so that they very possibly were due to other causes such as environmental pollutants rather than smoking. Moreover, even if epidemiological causation between smoking and the emergence of non-small-cell lung carcinomata and bronchioloalveolar carcinomata, which were non-specific diseases, could be acknowledged, the Court ruled, it was difficult to assert conclusively that the demonstration of the fact of a particular individual's smoking history and the fact of his or her development of non-specific diseases itself proved the probability of a causal relationship between the two facts.

To this date, cases regarding causation between smoking and cancer emergence have been addressed mainly in North American legal circles only. Consequently, there are many implications among international epidemiologists for the South Korean Supreme Court's recent judgment, which need to be addressed mainly in three aspects (Broadbent, 2015). For the sake of convenience, comments on the points of contention are provided in the order of the main points of the Court's written judgment.

First, the South Korean Supreme Court gave the verdict that, because the evils of smoking constituted a fact already and publicly acknowledged throughout society, tobacco companies did not have a special duty of notice above citizens' awareness of the evils of tobacco. According to South Korea's Product Liability Act, when making products that can cause risks to communities or individuals, manufacturers have a legal obligation to attach warning labels regarding evils that can emerge and to urge users' caution. However, the Supreme Court judged that it was adequate for tobacco companies to warn about the hazards of smoking through warning labels on tobacco packets. In a situation where the evils of tobacco have increased continuously in terms of public health, however, it is implausible that tobacco companies should be exempt from publicizing the ills of the product called tobacco themselves and from participating in such a social atmosphere. In the case of South Korea, tobacco price was increased by 2000 won from 2500 won to 4500 won in January 2015, and the attachment of pictorial cigarette warning labels to tobacco packets has been made mandatory from December 2016 through the revision of the National Health Promotion Act. Though somewhat belated in comparison with the South Korean government's ratification of the Framework Convention on Tobacco Control (FCTC) early on, such measures have been taken on the basis of the social consensus that the implementation of a full-fledged smoking cessation policy is necessary. Consequently, tobacco companies, too, must keenly feel their social responsibility and participate in the policy, especially in consideration of the strong toxicity of smoking and the increasingly low ages at which smokers initiate smoking. Moreover, even if the hazards of smoking are adequately known throughout society, credit for such achievements goes to professions in the field of public health including epidemiologists. In other words, the notification and promotion costs for risky products stipulated by laws including the Product Liability Act hitherto have been burdened mostly by the South Korean academia and government, and, taking advantage of this, tobacco companies engaged in business in the domestic market have been exempt from the health campaign costs that they themselves should shoulder and have obtained even higher rates of return. In its recent sentence, however, the Supreme Court did not hold tobacco companies responsible for such duty for public interest but, instead, drew the line regarding the duty of notice with respect to risks that these companies should assume, thus practically disregarding the many citizens suffering from diverse diseases due to tobacco addiction.

Second, the South Korean Supreme Court stated in its recent sentence that because smoking was a non-specific disease, the plaintiff must prove the argument that smoking was the only cause of lung cancer. In other words, the burden of proof was placed on the several cancer patients, the plaintiff. However, the Court's judgment in classifying diseases into specific diseases, due to particular causes, and non-specific diseases, due to multiple causes, seems to be far removed from the opinions of epidemiologists, who are the experts. The widely accepted theory in the academia today is that the causes of all diseases are fundamentally complex and that specificity is not an overwhelmingly important cause in the causal inference of disease emergence (Rothman, 1976). Of course, the emergence of certain diseases is premised on particular causes, and cases where those causes are not fulfilled can be seen as other diseases (Broadbent, 2009). For example, when Vibrio cholerae carriers exhibit symptoms of diarrhea, it is possible to infer that diarrhea is caused by the cholera germ (Broadbent & Hwang, 2016). Consequently, diarrhea not accompanied by the cholera germ is not indicative of cholera. Citing such an example, the Supreme Court would classify cholera as a specific disease. Even for a specific disease, however, separate demonstration is necessary regarding whether that disease is due to the particular cause in question. In other words, epidemio-logically speaking, the possibility of the existence of other causes of diarrhea cannot be ruled out. When hypothetical cases are under discussion, deductive reasoning is used. When explaining the mechanisms of disease emergence in reality, however, it is necessary to take into consideration the multiple causes of disease emergence in addition to an inductive reasoning process. Consequently, consistent research results that the relative risk of developing particular diseases is very high when an individual smokes must be adequately reviewed in law courts as well. If the probability of the emergence of lung cancer is very low for non-smokers but is very high for smokers, a causal relationship in disease emergence must be accepted even for non-specific diseases. The protection of victims can be considered more fairly when the causes of disease emergence are determined based on the results of studies conducted by mainstream epidemiologists instead of intuitive judgments on causal relationships according to the presence or absence of specificity.

Third, the greatest problem that has emerged from the South Korean Supreme Court's recent sentence is an attitude that, while treating the levels of judging scientific and statistical causation and legal causation as separate, denies epidemi-ological evidence regarding the relationship between tobacco and lung cancer emergence in law courts. Of course, the majority of legal literature has addressed how difficult it is to have causation acknowledged in individual-level cases based on statistical evidence concerning populations (Broadbent, 2011; Gold, 1986; Wright, 2008). Consequently, it is difficult to view the Supreme Court's stance as peculiar because of its recent judgment. Nevertheless, it is deeply regrettable that, amidst an increase in similar lawsuits, the Court did not cite epidemiological evi-dence even in its recent sentence. Not all fields of jurisprudence disregard statistical evidence, and those including forensic medicine have a considerably wide scope in acknowledging such evidence. Considering these facts, the Supreme Court's recent judgment can be seen as the product of a lack of understanding of specifying causal relationships based on epidemiological evidence.

According to the position of mainstream epidemiologists, epidemiological evidence must be applied to legal judgments in tobacco lawsuits for the following reasons (Broadbent & Hwang, 2016). Let us hypothesize that, in a certain population, there is a male smoking group whose members have smoked 20 or more cigarettes per day for over 30 years. In addition, if these members' relative risk of developing lung cancer is calculated to be 20 in comparison with that for non-smokers, the excess fraction of the smoking group's risk of developing lung cancer is $1 - (1/20) = 19/20$, or 0.95. This highly probable figure is obtained after adjusting the diverse sociodemographic characteristics of the individuals to be considered. Consequently, if lung cancer patients emerge from the smoking group after 10 years, it is possible to infer that the cause of the disease lies in smoking. It is because when calculations are made based on the figure above, the probability of smokers randomly sampled not from the lung cancer patient group but from the control group developing lung cancer only amounts to 5%. This is identical to the probability when smokers not belonging to the excess fraction of 95% are selected. Of course, because the etiological fraction can be greater than the excess fraction, smoking can be a contributable factor of lung cancer emergence (Greenland & Robins, 2000). Consequently, a causal relationship between smoking and lung cancer cannot be immediately proven through randomly selected particular cases. In other words, because epidemiological evidence only tracks the eventual differences between disparate groups, epidemiological evidence cannot be used to derive equations for obtaining causal probability. However, if differences between the two groups in incidence rates arise from smoking exposure, then it is possible to infer from numerous cases that the act of smoking serves as a cause of the emergence of lung cancer. Because the etiological fraction can be greater than the excess fraction, the probability of such an inference can be greater than but cannot be smaller than the actual fact (this can be expressed as the following inequation (Broadbent, 2013: 162–181). Of course, because law courts must reflect specific individuals' characteristics such as family histories and occupations, the inequation does not represent the minimum threshold level for the admissibility of evidence of epidemiological evidence). Through such an inference, if and when a particular hypothesis has been fulfilled, it is possible to derive probable conclusions for individual cases based on epidemiological evidence (Broadbent, 2011). This is no different from methods that are customarily used in criminal courts to derive probable conclusions regarding the possibility of the defendants' commitment of crimes. Regrettably, however, legal circles still remain inadequate in their understanding of associations between epidemiological evidence and particular causal relationships and have charged individuals with greater responsibility for disease emergence. Law courts are lenient toward manufacturers of tobacco, whose toxicity is equivalent to that of drugs, but are very parsimonious about protecting citizens who have developed lung cancer after consuming tobacco, such a dangerous product. How, then, should law courts' judgments on causal relationships and selective adoption of evidence be understood?

$$PC \geq 1 - \frac{1}{RR}$$

In conclusion, the South Korean Supreme Court's recent sentence is regrettable in that it went against the tendency in the jurisdictions of North America including Canada increasingly to charge tobacco companies with greater responsibility. This is because the verdict, instead of earnestly deliberating on the issue of acknowledging causal relationships in individual-level cases through epidemiological evidence, actually reduced the obligations of tobacco companies instead, with the Product Liability Act as a shield. Moreover, in considering lung cancer as a specific disease based on a misunderstanding of the mechanisms of disease emergence, the sentence failed to face directly the problem of damages due to chronic diseases, which have increased in high-level risk society. If the logic of the recent Supreme Court sentence is expanded, it will become impossible for citizens to be adequately protected against diverse health-related risk factors that can be caused by private enterprises. For example, all lawsuits filed by individuals regarding diseases due to fine dust, fast food, genetically modified organisms (GMOs), and excess food additives and castor sugar—which are called "negative external effects" in economics—such as respiratory ailments, obesity, adult diseases, and diabetes will inevitably be dismissed for the reason that they cannot prove causal relationships. Such sentences are a far cry from scientifically conventional wisdom. The South Korean judiciary therefore must review epidemiological evidence more closely and objectively in individual-level cases claiming compensation for damages and must study legal principles that are capable of determining the probability of the existence of causal relationships. Otherwise, judgments on legal causal relationships will inevitably become even further removed from the reality, and the relief of victims and the benefits and protections of laws will exist in name only.

References

Broadbent, A. (2009). Causation and models of disease in epidemiology. *Studies in History and Philosophy of Biological and Biomedical Sciences, 40,* 302–311.

Broadbent, A. (2011). Epidemiological evidence in proof of specific causation. *Legal Theory, 17,* 237–278.

Broadbent, A. (2013). *Philosophy of epidemiology (New directions in the philosophy of science).* New York: Palgrave Macmillan.

Broadbent, A. (2015). Epidemiological evidence in law: A comment on Supreme Court decision 2011Da22092 South Korea. *Epidemiology and Health, 37,* e2015025.

Broadbent, A., & Hwang, S. S. (2016). Tobacco and epidemiology in Korea: Old tricks, new answers? *Journal of Epidemiology and Community Health, 70*(6), 527–528.

Burton, P. R., Tobin, M. D., & Hopper, J. L. (2005). Key concepts in genetic epidemiology. *Lancet, 366*(9489), 941–951.

Davey Smith, G. (2011). Epidemiology, epigenetics and the 'Gloomy Prospect': Embracing randomness in population health research and practice. *International Journal of Epidemiology, 40*(3), 537–562.

Doll, R., & Hill, A. B. (1954). The mortality of doctors in relation to their smoking habits: A preliminary report. *British Medical Journal, 1*(4877), 1451–1455.

Gold, S. (1986). Causation in toxic torts: Burdens of proof, standards of persuasion, and statistical evidence. *Yale Law Journal, 96*, 376–402.

Greenland, S., & Robins, J. (2000). Epidemiology, justice, and the probability of causation. *Jurimetrics, 40*, 321–340.

Hill, G., Millar, W., & Connelly, J. (2003). The great debate 1: Smoking, lung cancer, and cancer epidemiology. *Canadian Bulletin of Medical History, 20*(2), 367–386.

Hong, Y. P., Kim, S. J., Lew, W. J., Lee, E. K., & Han, Y. C. (1998). The seventh nationwide tuberculosis prevalence survey in Korea, 1995. *International Journal of Tuberculosis Lung Diseases, 2*(1), 27–36.

Kim, D. S. (2010). Introduction: Health of the health care system in Korea. *Social Work in Public Health, 25*, 127–141.

Kim, K. S., & Lee, Y. J. (2010). Developments and general features of national health insurance in Korea. *Social Work in Public Health, 25*, 142–157.

Lee, S. G. (2016). Proving causation with epidemiological evidence in tobacco lawsuits. *Journal of Preventive Medicine and Public Health, 49*, 80–96.

Lee, S.-Y., Chun, C. B., Lee, Y. G., & Seo, N. K. (2008). The National Health Insurance system as one type of new typology: The case of South Korea and Taiwan. *Health Policy, 85*, 105–113.

Lichtenstein, P., Holm, N. V., Verkasalo, P. K., Iliadou, A., Kaprio, J., Koskenvuo, M., et al. (2000). Environmental and heritable factors in the causation of cancer—analyses of cohorts of twins from Sweden, Denmark, and Finland. *New England Journal of Medicine, 343*(2), 78–85.

Park, S., Jee, S. H., Shin, H. R., Park, E. H., Shin, A., Jung, K. W., et al. (2014). Attributable fraction of tobacco smoking on cancer using population-based nationwide cancer incidence and mortality data in Korea. *BMC Cancer, 14*, 406.

Pearce, N. (2011). Epidemiology in a changing world: Variation, causation and ubiquitous risk factors. *International Journal of Epidemiology, 40*(2), 503–512.

Peto, R., Darby, S., Deo, H., Silcocks, P., Whitley, E., & Doll, R. (2000). Smoking, smoking cessation, and lung cancer in the UK since 1950: Combination of national statistics with two case-control studies. *British Medical Journal, 321*(7257), 323–329.

Plomin, R. (2011). Why are children in the same family so different? Non-shared environment three decades later. *International Journal of Epidemiology, 40*, 582–592.

Proctor, R. N. (2012). The history of the discovery of the cigarette-lung cancer link: Evidentiary traditions, corporate denial, global toll. *Tobacco Control, 21*(2), 87–91.

Rothman, K. J. (1976). Causes. *American Journal of Epidemiology, 104*, 587–592.

Rothman, K. J., Greenland, S., & Lash, T. L. (Eds.). (2008). *Modern epidemiology* (3rd ed.). New York: Lippincott Williams & Wilkins.

Rutter, T. (1997). Tobacco companies seek to pay $300bn as lawsuit settlement. *British Medical Journal, 314*(7089), 1217.

Wright, R. (2008). Liability for possible wrongs: Causation, statistical probability, and the burden of proof. *Loyola Los Angeles Law Review, 41*, 1295–1344.

Wu-Williams, A. H., & Samet, J. M. (2000). Lung cancer and cigarette in the UK since 1950: Combination of national statistics with two case-control studies. *British Medical Journal, 321*, 323–329.

Wynder, E. L., Graham, E. A., & Croninger, A. B. (1953). Experimental production of carcinoma with cigarette tar. *Cancer Research, 13*(12), 855–864.

Chapter 5
Criteria of Epidemiological Causation and Its Limitations

Abstract The causal probability produced by epidemiology is meaningful for inferring the probability of causal relations because it indicates the probability of the development of particular diseases among patients randomly selected from populations due to the harmful factor in question and is a rational index that converts probability on the level of populations into probability on the level of individuals, or members. According to the results of epidemiological research accumulated over the past 50 years, the relative risk of developing lung cancer ranges from minimally two times as high to maximally 20 times as high for smokers in comparison with lifelong non-smokers. Moreover, because the harmful factors of disease development are constructive causes except for a few infectious diseases, specific relationships can be established for non-infectious diseases as well when the attributable fraction exceeds a particular figure. According to the results of a massive analysis of the data of South Korea's National Health Insurance Service (NHIS), when a patient with a particular type of lung cancer has a history of smoking of several decades of pack years, smoking can be seen as a cause of the development of the cancer in question. Of course, causal relations cannot be established with certainty based on partial information or figures, as also indicated by the epidemiological standards for determining causal relations, also referred to as Bradford Hill's criteria for causation. However, epidemiological evidence today supports the fact that long-term smoking can in fact cause lung cancer singly.

5.1 Criteria of Epidemiological Causation

In epidemiology, analyses are done to determine a causal relationship when an association is observed among phenomena or events even after adjusting for confounders, and the causality judgment criteria mainly used at such times are Hill's criteria (Gordis, 2013: 243–261). Created in the process through which the US Department of Health, Education, and Welfare (present-day Department of Health and Human Services) judged the association between smoking and lung cancer in

© The Author(s), under exclusive licence to Springer Nature Singapore Pte Ltd., part of Springer Nature 2018

M. Jung, *An Investigation of the Causal Inference Between Epidemiology and Jurisprudence*, SpringerBriefs in Philosophy, https://doi.org/10.1007/978-981-10-7862-0_5

1964, they are used as the universal criteria for causality judgment in epidemiology today (Rothman, 2012: 38–68). Examined specifically, these criteria are as follow:

Temporality of the Association: This is the principle that, in order to see a particular factor as the cause of a particular disease, exposure to that factor must occur before the onset of the disease. In other words, it is the principle that exposure to a risk factor must occur temporally before the onset of the disease in question. As a necessary condition for causality judgment, this principle is applied also in courts to prove a causal relationship between the incidence of a disease in a particular individual and exposure to a risk factor suspected of being the cause of the disease. In particular, when a latent period has been medically determined between the exposure and the disease, the credibility in inferring a causal relationship can be strengthened. However, the criteria above are usually applied to acute diseases because chronic diseases have complex onset mechanisms and long latent periods. In other words, it is possible to conclude that a causal relationship exists based on the temporality of the association when an acute disease develops after exposure to a particular risk factor and such an association is observed even after excluding other suspicious factors. On the other hand, the temporal interval between exposure and the disease is important as well when the temporality of the association is used as a causal criterion. For example, although asbestos is clearly related to an increase in the risk of lung cancer, the time taken from exposure to asbestos to the onset of lung cancer amounts to at least 15–20 years (Gordis, 2013: 243–261). Therefore, when a person develops lung cancer five years after exposure to asbestos, exposure to asbestos must be excluded from possible causes of the disease.

Strength of the Association: The strength of an association is measured by using the relative risk or the odds ratio, and the stronger the association is, the more likely the relationship is to be causal. For example, when the relative risk amounts to 10.0, such a result is very unlikely to be due to biases or confounders. Consequently, a causal association is assumed to exist between the two. However, because the possibility of the result being due to an unadjusted factor must be taken into consideration when the relative risk amounts to 1.2, it is difficult to state conclusively that a causal relationship exists even though such a relationship is not negated.

Biological Probability: This is the case for which the relationship among observed phenomena coheres with existing biological knowledge. Of course, it is not necessary to discard all data just because they do not cohere with biological knowledge at the time of the research. This is because epidemiological observations can be ahead of biological knowledge. For example, Gregg's observations of rubella and congenital cataract in the mid-twentieth century were discoveries surpassing contemporary biological knowledge of deformed viruses (McAlister Gregg, 2001).

Repeatability: In nearly no case is a causal relationship settled on with a single epidemiological study. Academia accepts a causal relationship only when an association is consistently observed also in other studies on different populations conducted by other researchers. However, this criterion is rarely used for legal judgment in actual lawsuits because repeated research results are often insufficient.

Dose–response Relationships: When an increase in the degree of exposure to a factor that causes a disease leads to an increase in the incidence rate of the disease, this is called a dose–response relationship. For example, the age-adjusted mortality rate due to tracheal cancer increases according to the amount of cigarettes smoked (Hammond & Horn, 1984). Though this relationship becomes a strong basis for inferring a causal relationship when it is observed, its absence does not negate causality. For example, when there exists a threshold value, the related disease does not develop up to a certain level of exposure to a risk factor but does develop once the threshold value has been exceeded.

Exposure Termination Effect: When a particular factor is the cause of a disease, reduced exposure to that factor reduces the risk of the disease. For example, eosinophilia–myalgia syndrome (EMS) was rampant in the USA at the end of the 1980s. This disease, which is characterized by extreme myalgia and an increase in the number of blood eosinophils, was discovered to be related to the prescription of L-tryptophan. When the US Food and Drug Administration (FDA) prohibited the nonprescription compounding of this medicine, cases of EMS decreased dramatically (Swygert et al., 1990). Consequently, the termination of exposure becomes strong evidence supporting a causal association. However, this criterion cannot be applied if data on the effect of terminating exposure cannot be obtained. In addition, the termination of exposure cannot block the onset in the case of irreversible diseases. For example, although smoking does not lead to recovery from pneumothorax, it can slow down the progress of the disease.

Coherence of the Association: When a relationship is causal, the results will cohere with other knowledge as well. However, the likelihood of a causal relationship decreases when the association is strong but does not cohere with knowledge other than biological or medical knowledge. For example, when the lung cancer incidence rate increases despite a decrease in cigarette sales, a causal relationship between smoking and lung cancer cannot be inferred until the reasons for the phenomenon have been explained rationally.

Possibility of Other Explanations: A causal relationship cannot be inferred when the association from the data is a result of biases or confounders.

Specificity of the Association: When a 1:1 association exists between a particular disease and a risk factor, this is called a specific relationship, and causality is likely to exist between the two. However, causality can be acknowledged even in cases without the specificity of the association if the phenomena in question can be explained rationally and biologically. For example, an argument has been presented that because smoking is related to various diseases including pancreatic cancer, heart diseases, pulmonary emphysema, and bladder cancer, the specificity of the association does not exist between smoking and lung cancer and a causal relationship therefore cannot be acknowledged. However, there is no problem with inferring a causal relationship if the association between harmful ingredients in cigarettes and the diseases listed above can be explained biologically.

5.2   Critiques of the Epidemiological Criteria

While inferring causal relationships with particular lists like Hill's criteria is a method commonly used in epidemiological circles, there also exist critical opinions (Rothman, 2012: 38–68). In other words, the argument is that because each element of Hill's criteria is vague or limited in its scope of application, the temporality of an association is in fact the only significant criterion. When a list like Hill's criteria is created to infer causal relationships, it is possible to overestimate elements included on the list and to underestimate those excluded from the list. Consequently, Hill's criteria must be seen not as an absolute reference but as a list of diverse elements that can be taken into consideration. In other words, it cannot be stated conclusively that a causal relationship either exists just because all of the criteria above have been met or does not exist just because a particular element has not been met (Egilman, Kim, & Biklen, 2003). Judges must bear this in mind in the process of judging the credibility of the results of epidemiological studies or evidence adoption in courts. Although what we call "scientific knowledge" may seem to explain all existing phenomena, it is in fact an aggregate of still unrefuted hypotheses.

When it is considered difficult to prove causality based on partial epidemiological evidence, a causal relationship can be inferred by synthesizing the results of existing studies and calculating the odds ratio. This is called a meta-analysis. Meta-analyses are accepted as an appropriate method mainly in experimental studies because it presupposes a strict study design where study subjects are randomly assigned to disparate case groups (Greenberg, Daniels, Flanders, Eley, & Boring, 2005). Consequently, there are debates regarding the appropriateness of meta-analyses for observational studies (Stroup et al., 2000). This is because differences in results can arise due to chance when study subjects are not randomly assigned.

5.3   Pragmatic Pluralism in Causal Inference

To acknowledge that smoking is a cause of lung cancer, epidemiological evidence and clinical and pathological evidence related to causality were discussed since the mid-twentieth century (Bird, 2011). Consequently, in the fields of the philosophy of science and the philosophy of law, there has arisen a position that seeks to limit the definition of *causality* in addition to the analysis of causal inference using methods such as counterfactual reasoning (Hernan & Robins, 2015). Those who support this position argue that randomized controlled trials (RCTs) are the only outstanding methods to evaluate causality and that observational studies are significant only to reproduce RCT (Hernan, 2005). A strong position regarding causality in the philosophy of law comes from the potential outcome approach (POA), which makes it difficult to provide relief to victims by increasing the use of epidemiological evidence in courts (Imbens & Rubin, 2015: 23–43). Consequently, the present study evaluates the fundamental issues in relation to causal inference and the problems that are inherent in the restricted potential outcome approach (RPOA), which is a position that seeks to limit the POA. In addition, it discusses pragmatic pluralism in legal causal inference as an alternative.

5.3.1 Potential Outcome Approach

The potential outcome approach (POA) shares many qualities with counterfactual conceptions of causation found in traditional analytic philosophy (Lewis, 1973a, b). The POA always implies that the effect of an exposure is measured relative to some contrary-to-fact condition. It has been likened to the counterfactual analysis of causation briefly proposed by David Hume. However, for example, meaningful causal inferences cannot be drawn from obesity because well-defined interventions are a necessary condition for measuring causal effects (Hernan & Taubman, 2008).

The core of the contemporary POA is the idea that, in order to make a meaningful causal claim, one must clearly specify the intervention one has in mind to bring about a difference between the exposed group and the unexposed group. POA insists that investigators clearly specify counterfactuals whose truth they are investigating. Additionally, the POA is often thought to imply a kind of rank among study designs, with experimental studies coming out well, because in such studies investigators actually engage in an intervention to create exposed and control groups. A well-specified intervention is causally uniform in that it has the same effect on the outcome of interest in different cases.

An intervention that reduces obesity does not satisfy this criterion with respect to the outcome mortality due to the different ways in which one might reduce obesity and so have different effects on mortality. However, in this example, it is not enough to merely investigate the effects of obesity on mortality. There are many ways to intervene so as to reduce (or increase) body mass index (BMI), and these may have different effects on mortality (Hernan & Taubman, 2008). Exercise and diet may have different effects; smoking or amputation could reduce BMI, which is used to measure obesity, but is likely to have quite different effects on mortality from either exercise or diet. This means that if one conducts a study on the association between obesity and mortality, one cannot make reliable claims of the potential outcomes of a decrease in obesity in the study population and this would depend on how obesity was decreased. Proponents of this line of reasoning argue that this inability to identify the potential outcome–the inability to assert a counterfactual–means that such a study is not well-placed to provide evidence for a causal inference.

Modern epidemiologists are usually concerned with studies confirming or falsifying general causal claims such as that smoking causes cancer (Rothman, 1976) —not true for the contemporary analytic philosopher. Philosophers of science and metaphysicians working with counterfactual conceptions of causation are more often interested in well-specified token events, and this is exemplified by Hume's doctrine that one event causes another where if the first object had not been, the second never existed (Hume, 1975)—let us call this approach the Lewisian conception. The distinction between the singular and general causal claims seems to have gone unnoticed in epidemiology literature. Thus, ties between Hume and Lewis's conditional or counterfactual accounts and the epidemiologists' POA have been grossly exaggerated (Lewis, 1973b). Nevertheless, the proponents of the POA adopt a similar strategy to the Lewisian conception in that they judge causal effects based not only on the actual outcomes of a patient's actual exposure, but also on the potential outcomes of alternative, unrealized exposures on the same patients. Therefore, assigning the phrase counterfactual account seems appropriate to both the Lewisian conception and the POA (Lewis, 2000).

The POA also insists that investigators clearly specify the counterfactuals whose truths they are investigating. Additionally, the POA also often thought to imply a kind of ranking among study designs, with experimental studies coming out well, because in such studies, the investigators actually make an intervention to create the exposed and control groups. A well-specified intervention is causally uniform in that it has the same effect on the outcome of interest in different cases. An intervention that reduces obesity does not satisfy this criterion with respect to the outcome *mortality* because the different ways in which one might reduce obesity have different effects on mortality.

Epidemiology is a prescriptive discipline that is directed at improving public health through group studies. Given its prescriptive nature, prima facie epidemiologists only need to be concerned with manipulable conditions—if one cannot prevent a condition from being satisfied and if one cannot interfere with a condition as a form of treatment, one may as well consider it causally redundant. For example, it would be odd to consider "being male" a cause of testicular cancer, even though only males contract the disease and many of those who consider the POA to be a conception of causation would argue that this is because "being male" is a non-manipulable condition in the population susceptible to the disease. However, to study the relationship between testosterone levels and testicular cancer, testosterone levels can be interfered with. On the face of it, information concerning causal relationships between manipulable conditions like testosterone levels and diseases is, unlike information about non-manipulable conditions like "being male," useful when making public health policies. One cannot make claims about causal effects without specifying at least one well-defined intervention (Hernan & Taubman, 2008).

The POA is ultimately an attempt to outline the necessary and sufficient conditions for causes, and Lewis's proposal is straight forward: put simply, some token event X causes some token event Y only if X makes a difference; i.e., if both X and Y occur, and if, in a possible world identical to the actual world until the moment X occurs, X was not to occur and the world was left to evolve according to the laws of nature of the actual world, then Y would not occur. This conception alone is of little use to the epidemiologist. Of course, moving from just a single causal inference of the kind identified by the Lewisian method to general causal inferences about the effects of actions like smoking, immunization, and exercise would clearly be unjustified (Lewis, 2000), and there is no room for debate here. However, as we have noticed, there is a lack of clear thinking about prediction and about the way causal knowledge can be used to predict, as we will see in the next section—both within epidemiology and much more broadly. This is misguided because the POA sets the generation of useful predictions as a necessary condition for a causal claim to be well-formulated.

5.3.2 Restricted Potential Outcome Approach

The RPOA originates from a pragmatic attitude toward causality adopted by epidemiologists who study smoking and lung cancer. It is reasonable to borrow the concept of pragmatic causality from medicine and public health. The main reason to elucidate the pathological elements of human diseases is to prevent disease. If the incidence rates of a particular disease decrease as exposure to a particular element decreases, then that element is a cause of the disease under question (Lilienfeld, 1957). Consequently, the position that supports the RPOA emphasizes that the *cash value* must increase by limiting causality to cases where human intervention is possible. Taking a strong attitude toward causality, the POA is used together with counterfactual thinking that is not accompanied by interventions (Rothman, Greenland, & Lash, 2008: 54). However, the POA is used even when discussing RCT or hypothetical interventions (Rothman et al., 2008: 59). Here, the POA is referred to as the RPOA because it has a limited nature. Although it is important for teaching and practicing epidemiology, causal inference based on the RPOA limits even the scope of acceptable evidence during causality evaluations, thus hindering reasonable causal inference during the public health decision-making process.

The RPOA differs from the POA in two aspects. First, for the RPOA, interventions and manipulation must be humanly feasible. Next, the RPOA considers causal claims that cannot be predicted in hypothetical scenarios as being unless (Halpern & Pearl, 2005). Of course, there also exists causation that is not accompanied by manipulation. Race leads to discrimination, and disparate hormones are secreted according to biological sex. Nature is a phenomenon that determines the value of specific variables and does not require human manipulation (Pearl, 2009: 361–368).

For causation to be affected, responsiveness, or the ability of a particular variable to react to changes in another variable, is indispensable; however, the causes of changes are not important (Morgan, 2013: 313). For this reason, scientists have devised a concept of counterfactuals, which describe situations where the state of the conditions precedents is realized even without specifying the physical means.

The characteristics of the RPOA are as follows. First, predictions through causal inference in hypothetical scenarios are allowed. Second, causal conditions and interventions must be properly stipulated. Third, determining the causality is limited only to causal conditions and interventions thus stipulated. Fourth, observational studies must be as similar as possible to the conditions of experimental studies that make use of the RCT. Causation can be reasonably inferred only when such conditions have been satisfied (Hernan & Taubman, 2008). However, to define a particular causal effect properly, counterfactual outcomes must be meticulously defined. In other words, a broad consensus on relevant interventions is necessary (Hernan, 2005). Interventions are actions that humans can theoretically take, and contrasting or non-actual situations can arise due to human interventions.

The RPOA is a part of a universal philosophical analysis, and it is useful when epidemiologists ponder causality. Such usefulness is based on the predictive value of causal claims related to specifically stipulated interventions. When positivistic associations that have been elucidated by statistical analyses in the fields of observational epidemiology and social sciences are observed, it is reasonably possible to speculate through particular covariates what will happen to a certain person in the future. However, such associations do not take into consideration the predictions in counterfactual scenarios (VanderWeele & Hernan, 2012). In the end, the goal of the RPOA is to make accurate predictions regarding counterfactual scenarios where causal claims can be generated by particular interventions or manipulations.

The RPOA considers causal claims superior to associational claims. If so, then does causal inference consist of estimating an improperly defined causal effect or calculating the relative risk estimates? Dominating the statistics and the social sciences, causal inference today is commonly understood in terms of contrast in counterfactual outcomes. It generally consists of certain human actions that give rise to counterfactuals (VanderWeele, 2015: pp. 452–455). In the 1970s-80s, philosophers strove to clearly define counterfactuals and to use them in causation analysis (Lewis, 1973a, b). In addition, links between philosophical thinking and statistical thinking regarding causation were gradually created (Pearl, 2009; Spirtes, Glymour, & Scheines, 1993: 19–58). Philosophers have discussed about in-depth semantic interpretations of the concept of counterfactuals (Lewis, 2001). In contrast, epidemiologists are interested in the epistemology of counterfactuals, or in determining how counterfactuals lead to causality evaluations. For these reasons, the term "potential outcomes" is often preferred because it allows one to avoid the philosophical complexity of possible worlds (Greenland, 1999).

Issues that are created in courts generally concern observational study situations outside the laboratories. Consequently, it is impossible to satisfy RCT conditions or to perform manipulations in experimental study situations. Observational studies, therefore, are considered RCT only when they satisfy the following conditions: First, the effects of the treatments compared correspond to well-defined interventions. Second, the conditional probability of the effects of all treatments is not determined by researchers but is changed only according to the measured covariates. Third, the conditional probability of the effects of all treatments is a positive (+) value greater than 0 (Hernan & Robins, 2015). In fact, the RPOA belongs to the set of difference-making theories of causation (Beebee, Hitchcock, & Menzies, 2009: 158–183). According to difference-making theories of causation, a cause is an event that leads to differences in the outcome. If the cause was different, then the outcome would likewise be different, and if the cause did not exist, then the event itself would not occur. These differences between the cause and the outcome have resulted into several genealogies. The first theory is the traditional counterfactual theory (Lewis, 1973b). One example is the proposition that a person would not have suffered myocardial infarction if he or she had not been obese. The second theory is contrastivism, which argues for a quadrilateral relationship among the cause, the outcome, contrast for the cause, and contrast for the effect (Schaffer, 2005). Third, interventionism is a position that sees causation as being completed through certain interventions (Woodward, 2003: p. 20). For example, if an obese person were to receive an exercise prescription in order to reduce weight, then that person's myocardial infarction incidence rate would decrease.

The contrastivistic perspective and the interventionistic perspective differ from the counterfactual perspective owing to semantics, which controls counterfactual conditionals (Woodward, 2003: pp. 23–25). The RPOA belongs to the interventionistic group. In fact, interventionism is classified into two types. First, in-principle interventionism does not limit interventions to humanly feasible ones. Although humans cannot generate earthquakes, earthquakes clearly are interventions. Next, humanly feasible interventionism is a position arguing that actually humanly feasible interventions correspond to causes, thus defining interventions narrowly. In epidemiology, the RPOA belongs to none other than this category. The POA belongs to the set of either counterfactual approaches or interventionistic approaches depending on which version of POA is applied (VanderWeele & Robinson, 2014). In contrast, the RPOA supports humanly feasible interventionism and considers causality to be evaluable only with RCT. However, when this approach is applied to all situations judged as causal, there arises a dilemma where risks increase epidemiologically and the probability of being able to state which theory is philosophically correct decreases (Rothman, 2014).

5.3.3 Difficult Points of RPOA

The RPOA has many problems; they may be philosophical or epidemiological. First, in determining causality, the RPOA cannot appropriately respond to the problem of unfeasible interventions (VanderWeele & Robinson, 2014). In RPOA theorists' view, it is difficult to conceptualize or to quantify the nonexistence of a certain feasible intervention that can change causation. However, there are two counterarguments. First, the boundary of humanly feasible interventions is unclear. This boundary can change with the passage of time. Until the emergence of statins, which are cholesterol-lowering agents, hypercholesteremia was pointed out as a cause of cardiovascular disorders (Stamler & Neaton, 2008). Although humans cannot currently intervene in the two causes of breast cancer 1 (BRCA1) and breast cancer 2 (BRCCA2), they will be able to do so someday. Next, the RPOA confounds what humans can conceptualize and what they can actually execute. In the POA, an intervention does not necessarily have to be feasible in order to be specified as a precondition of causal inference.

Second, the RPOA cannot appropriately respond to "states" such as obesity as causes. In observational studies, one is not aware of the process through which the body mass index (BMI) of each experimental subject has reached 20. Consequently, because the counterfactual outcome is vague, no causal contrast that is accompanied by the outcome can be properly defined (Hernan & Taubman, 2008). If "states" such as obesity are no longer considered as causes, then the epidemiologists will be pursuing only interventions instead of pathological elements.

Third, the RPOA is based on the concept of well-specified interventions, which deals with whether or not an intervention is humanly feasible. When it has been decided that the BMI values of a group of obese people are to be lowered, the effect on the mortality rates of group members will differ according to the intervention method (e.g., exercise prescription, liposuction) (Hernan & Taubman, 2008). In this case, it cannot be claimed that 100,000 people lose their lives to obesity every year. Instead, the phrasing should be that 50,000 people can avoid death through dietary treatments and that liposuction is not helpful. Consequently, obesity is not a well-specified cause, and overeating, a lack of exercise, or both are well-specified causes. Here, the problem is that an overall definition of well-specified interventions is necessary. The claim that causation is well-specified only in cases where interventions are well-specified creates many problems. First, in many cases, it is difficult to know in advance whether or not a certain intervention has been properly specified (Broadbent, 2015a, b). Next, there are cases in which, despite the fact that the goals of an intervention have been achieved, the precise essence of that particular intervention does not seem very important (Staessen, Wang, & Thijs, 2001).

One of the central argumentative methods for defending a particular hypothesis in science is to grasp the most persuasive alternative hypothesis and to look for evidence that will exclude that alternative hypothesis. Inference to the best explanation places methods for excluding competing hypotheses at the heart of scientific reasoning (Lipton, 2004a, b). The strategy of causal inference and prediction in the epidemiological model likewise stress reaching a stable outcome through the exclusion of alternative hypotheses (Broadbent, 2013: 26–55). The exclusion of alternative hypotheses is an important method for evaluating a particular hypothesis. If an important alternative hypothesis is compatible with the available evidence, then questions have not yet been answered—even when that piece of evidence presents experimental evidence. However, if only a single hypothesis can explain all pieces of evidence, then the questions have been resolved even when those pieces of evidence present observational evidence.

In the end, the perspective from which the RPOA views the essence of causality is excessively limited. The most important critique of the RPOA is that it ranks evidence while disregarding, in effect, the contextual dependence of the evidence. Although a single piece of evidence is meager for use in itself as evidence of causality, it can play a key role in a large structure that will serve as a strong basis for causality. This is related to the fact that the constitutional hypothesis, according to which the emergence of smoking and lung cancer is constitutionally linked, has not been accepted for some time. This hypothesis can be rebutted only by conducting RCT that assess smoking over a long time, from the youth to old age of the experimental subjects (Vandenbroucke, 2009). When monozygotic twins were assessed in analytical epidemiological studies, the incidence rates of the lung cancer incidence rates in smokers from among twins were excessively high (Carmelli & Page, 1996). However, it was too late for these findings to affect the debates. Smoking started to spread widely during the first half of the twentieth century. The constitutional hypothesis claims that although people who were susceptible to lung cancer may have continued to smoke, this does not mean that the habit of smoking would have affected the genetic variations *associated* with an increasing risk of the emergence of lung cancer. Moreover, the claim that the degree to which lung cancer spreads would have increased in a short period due to genetic mutations is preposterous (Haack, 1998: 95). Consequently, the context of the evidence should be taken into consideration when evaluating causality; however, the RPOA overlooks this fact.

The RPOA makes use of diverse models in order to reach a single, comprehensive judgment through pieces of epidemiological evidence. First, triangulation is a model where the reliability of the results of a particular study increases when all diverse data and evidence consistently correspond to those results (Bryman, 2015). For example, when an analysis of propensity scores shows the same association as a certain instrumental variable analysis that is based on a very different hypothesis, the potential causation of that association is supported (Schneeweiss, Seeger, Landon, & Walker, 2008). Second, negative controls help to evaluate and to quantify competing explanations. Negative controls are largely classified into exposure controls and outcome controls (Lipsitch, Tchetgen Tchetgen, & Cohen, 2010). For example, in research on the effect of the habit of smoking on the results of pregnancy, the research results may be due to other characteristics of pregnant women who smoke. However, the fact that father's smoking is unrelated to the results of pregnancy supports the claim that infants and children with dysmorphic features (deformities) have been affected by smoking (Howe et al., 2012).

When epidemiological research draws evidence from other scientific fields, the interlocking of the evidence occurs. In order to determine causation between smoking and the emergence of lung cancer, carcinogens in tar in the case of chimney cleaners (observational studies), intraepithelial carcinoma and impaired endothelial functions of smokers' lungs (pathological approach), high volumes of cigarette tar detected on the skin (animal experiments), and other evidence are also examined in addition to epidemiological data (Vandenbroucke, 2009). Experimental evidence supplements epidemiological research well, and it is an important part of the overall evidence of causation. For example, the biochemical explanation that smoking is a cause of lung cancer is possible (Denissenko, Pao, Tang, & Pfeifer, 1996). Of course, causality cannot be proven with this alone. For causal inference, more information than data derived from particular studies is necessary, and messages from disparate scientific fields should be combined in a mutually supplementary manner.

The importance of context-based evidence and the fact that excluding alternatives is one of the central methods of causal inference have hitherto been discussed.

When triangulation techniques such as negative controls and the interlocking of the evidence are applied, very strong causal inference becomes possible through observational studies. The RPOA considers particular research designs and analyses as very important for causal inference, and it focuses on them. However, the RPOA cannot explain the value of bad evidence at a comprehensive level. It can neither present the methods for using triangulation or interlocking frameworks of evidence nor can it explain the power of such frameworks or the importance of excluding alternatives. Consequently, the perspective of the RPOA excessively limits the types of acceptable evidence, thus hindering reasonable causal inference (Pearce, 1996).

5.4 Scientific Evidence in the Court

Evidence obtained by using the scientific method, legal scientific evidence, generally refers to material evidence that is to be submitted to courts of law or evidence that has been collected by applying principles or techniques in the fields of particular academic disciplines or knowledge and that is tested or whose results are analyzed by experts or bearers of techniques in those fields (Lee, 2012). Scientific evidence must be understood in a manner that combines factual and normative aspects. From a factual aspect, experts in relevant fields can easily judge the reliability and validity of that evidence. From the normative aspect, the principles that serve as the basis of analysis include scientific grounds so that the results of judgments can be allowed as evidence in trials. A discussion of the requirements for scientific evidence to be presented in law courts and on the extent of judges' freedom of strong beliefs has emerged as an important issue today (Kim, 2012).

With the ability to contribute to fact-finding and the admissibility of evidence, the competence of evidence is legally related to natural relevance and is permitted in cases that do not involve prohibition on evidence use. Here, relevance signifies the degree of probability that can aid in making judgments on the factuality of evidence. With the development of fields concerning the collection of material evidence and the analysis of information included in such kind of evidence today, research on the theoretical validity of scientific evidence, appropriateness of concrete testing methods, and legal relevance have been conducted. Regarding evidentiary methods for example, the US Supreme Court considers DNA analysis results and graphology as meaningful circumstantial evidence and does not consider their advantages or disadvantages for the defendants (Kim, 2012). Law courts emphasize that the results of such analyses are just single statistical statements. Consequently, even if DNA evidence has probative power, it does not mean that the evaluation of all other evidentiary methods can be omitted.

The *Frye* standard played a pioneering role in evaluating the admissibility of scientific evidence. In *Frye v. United States* in 1923, the defendant demanded that lie detector tests be allowed to prove innocence.[1] Due to rejection of this demand by law courts, the scale of "general acceptance" in the so-called *Frye* standard came to be created. In accordance with this, lie detectors were evaluated as being untrustworthy and having failed to obtain general acceptance in relevant fields, or as being unreliable, at the time. Next, the *Daubert* standard served to present more developed standards for the admissibility of scientific evidence. In *Daubert v. Merrell Dow Pharmaceuticals, Inc.* in 1993, the US Supreme Court stated that judges of fact-finding proceedings must allow all scientific testimonies that were not only relevant but also reliable, thus presenting the so-called standards regarding relevance and reliability.[2] In other words, the Supreme Court stated that scientific knowledge should be the topic of expert appraisals and only then could the reliability of demonstrations be based on scientific validity. In fact, before the *Daubert* standard, misuse of scientific evidence was a serious problem in the American criminal judicature (Jasanoff, 1995: Chap. 3). According to reliability, which is the key content of the *Daubert* standard, judges of fact-finding proceedings should focus only on experts' principles and methodologies, and not on their results (Kim, 2012). Dealing with *Daubert v. Merrell Dow Pharmaceuticals, Inc.*, the US Supreme Court enumerated the following standards that need to be taken into consideration by judges of fact-finding proceedings: first, whether the theories or techniques had been reviewed or could be reviewed; second, whether those theories or techniques had been reviewed by peers or were made public; third, the known error rates for particular scientific techniques; fourth, standards regarding the use of the techniques; and fifth, the degree of acceptance of those techniques in related scientific communities. Consequently, the discretion of judges of fact-finding proceedings increased, and the controllability of reviews by appellate courts of appeals decreased dramatically.

Today, in cases where there is no illegality in the procedures for the acquisition of evidence and the evidence presented original evidence and its objective relevance is acknowledged, no special problem is raised regarding the competence of evidence (Kim, 2012). In the end, an increasingly dominant position examines the admissibility of evidence and the competence of evidence at the same time and emphasizes that scientific evidence has the competence of evidence when its means and methods are valid and reliable. This is linked to the position that because the competence of evidence must not be judged based on simple relevance and because the validity and appropriateness of scientific theories must be reviewed strictly, the requirement of reliability of scientific evidence must be added. If so, then what does the use of epidemiological evidence in law courts signify today?

First, according to the *Frye* test, which demands that anyone who is seeking to submit testimonies based on the scientific process should prove that such processes are generally approved in the fields under question, epidemiological evidence can be amply used in law courts (Jasanoff, 1995: Chap. 3). A unique methodology in

---

[1]Frye v. United States, 293 F. 1013 (D. C. Cir. 1923).
[2]Daubert v. Merrel Dow Pharmaceuticals, 509 U. S. 579 (1993).

public health with a history of over 150 years, epidemiology is customarily applied in fields of rudimentary medicine today, and clinicians also examine and treat patients based on epidemiological statistics. Along with prevalence rates and incidence rates, epidemiological indices such as odds ratios are used as very important grounds for judgments on clinical decisions.

Next, according to the *Daubert* test, epidemiological evidence must pass even more stringent reviews. As has been stated above, the US Supreme Court established the standards for the scientific admissibility of evidence in 1993 in *Daubert v. Merrell Dow Pharmaceuticals, Inc.*, which was related to epidemiologists' testimonies regarding the harmfulness of particular drugs (Jasanoff, 1995: Chap. 3). In accordance with these standards, there are five checklists regarding the legal usability of epidemiological evidence. First, is the evidence verifiable? If so, then has it been actually verified? Second, has the evidence been published in scientific journals and reviewed by peers? Third, what are the known or potential error rates for the methods used? Fourth, are there standards capable of controlling the experimental process? If so, then have such standards been used in the process of creating expert testimonies? Fifth, is the evidence accepted in related fields to a certain degree? To respond to the first and second standards, epidemiological evidence has been verified through countless epidemiological studies. In particular, in terms of the research methodology, epidemiological research exists in various forms ranging from cross-sectional studies to longitudinal cohort studies, and its competence of evidence increases substantially when randomized assignment is performed. Consequently, long-term prospective cohort research using randomized controlled trials (RCTs) has considerable competence of evidence in estimating causation in medical public health studies. Likewise, in tobacco lawsuits, the association between smoking and lung cancer is a conclusion derived by research papers published in professional academic journals that have been consistently verified for over 50 years since 1960 (Gordis, 2013: Chap. 12). Likewise, regarding the possibility of potential errors and control during the experimental process, which constitute the third standards, the epidemiological research methodology has developed in a sophisticated manner. As has been examined above, diverse biases are taken into consideration in the study design stage and confounding factors that can influence the cause and the effect are corrected during the statistical analysis process. Professional academic journals, wherein epidemiological papers are published, are equipped with systems for strictly verifying such errors and incorrect analyses. Finally, with respect to the general acceptance by and among the expert groups, which is the fifth standard, there are differences according to the issue. Nevertheless, the submission of expert statements by epidemiologists to law courts has become universal. For example, in relation to epidemiological investigations on lung diseases due to humidifier sterilizers, the Korean Society of Epidemiology (KSE) submitted a written response by experts to the Seoul Central District Prosecutors' Office in May 2016. Consequently, there is ample room for epidemiological research to pass the *Daubert* standard and to be used as meaningful scientific evidence in law courts, and this holds true also for tobacco lawsuits.

Of course, the limitations should also be examined. As discussed in criminal courts in recent years, brain imaging evidence cannot be easily used as a material for proving defendants' criminal responsibility. Moreover, making brain imaging mandatory for criminal defendants can violate the right to privacy or the right to one's body in response to search and seizure (Lee, 2012). Furthermore, the actual value of evidence cannot but decrease if and when causal inference according to scientific evidence is technically inaccurate in relation to probative power. However, one-sidedly and categorically denying scientific evidence that is advantageous for defendants can be disadvantageous for protecting victims' benefit and protection of the law. Consequently, it is necessary to appropriately reduce the possibility of an error in evidence through measures such as the shift in the burden of proof and to identify substantial truth (Jasanoff, 1995: Chap. 10). If so, population-level attributable fractions can be used as indirect evidence even in cases for relieving individual victims from tobacco lawsuits. Here, if and when tobacco companies, which are the defendants, cannot disprove the fact that the plaintiffs' lung cancer developed due to other factors, the plaintiffs' arguments can be accepted, and comparative negligence can be partly applied.

5.5 Remarks

It is not useful to adopt a firm philosophical position regarding the essence of causation in the philosophy of law or epidemiology. Pragmatic pluralism can be a realistic alternative. If the contexts of causation are judged with the help of counterfactualism and interventionism while epidemiological evidence is etiologically interpreted, "states" such as high blood pressure, hypercholesteremia, and diabetes mellitus can be presented as causal factors (Glymour & Glymour, 2014). Although the perspective of causal pluralism already exists, pragmatic pluralism is a combination of quietism regarding the essence of causation and pluralism regarding causal concepts (Hall, 2004: 225–276). While it is not the best tool for evaluating causality, the RPOA still has value when explaining causation-limited situations.

Occupying a dominant position in the field of theoretical epidemiology today, the causal inference movement was actually born through the combination of the counterfactual school, the interventionistic school, and the contrastivistic school with respect to causality. Causal inference is insufficient to serve as grounds for thinking about causality, as it does not take into consideration the fact that, to evaluate causality, diverse types of evidence must be combined. Though useful for resolving some complex epidemiological problems, newly emerging causal inference techniques cannot be used as an epidemiological foundation because they apply only to particular problems belonging to particular environments. Consequently, it is necessary to adopt pragmatic pluralism, which is rooted in the investigative process of searching for solutions to problems itself, rather than to hold onto the tenets of any particular school. Causal inference will continue to demonstrate characteristics that the RPOA does not capture or explain in the future.

This is the exclusion of alternative hypotheses through the interlocking of pictures that are larger than the sum of their parts.

For jurisprudentially and epidemiologically reasonable causal inference, all of the following must be taken into consideration: first, the fact that causal inference is a judgment based on the results of a combination of diverse types of evidence; second, strategies of excluding alternatives and firmly establishing causality through the task of interlocking triangulation, negative controls, and evidence drawn from other scientific fields; and third, components that do not match ideal counterfactual situations (Vandenbroucke & Pearce, 2015). In conclusion, the task of combining diverse types of knowledge will continue to be valid in the future. A study is but a clue to the background of particular evidence. Necessary are studies that are as diverse as possible. Akin to Bradford Hill's viewpoint, all possible evidence must be taken into consideration in order to make decisions on public health. It is scientifically invalid to limit epidemiology to a single RPOA paradigm given that the RPOA limits the scope of research to hypotheses where particular (hypothetical) interventions can be imagined. Consequently, it is desirable to adopt an open attitude while continuing to maintain a pluralistic perspective on causality evaluation.

References

Beebee, H., Hitchcock, C., & Menzies, P. (Eds.). (2009). *The Oxford handbook of causation*. Oxford, UK: Oxford University Press.

Bird, A. (2011). The epistemological function of Hill's criteria. *Preventive Medicine, 53*, 242–245.

Broadbent, A. (2013). *Philosophy of epidemiology (new directions in the philosophy of science)*. New York, NY: Palgrave Macmillan.

Broadbent, A. (2015a). Epidemiological evidence in law: A comment on Supreme Court Decision 2011Da22092. *South Korea. Epidemiology and Health, 37*, e2015025.

Broadbent, A. (2015b). Causation and prediction in epidemiology: A guide to the 'methodological revolution'. *Studies in History and Philosophy of Biological and Biomedical Sciences, 54*, 72–80.

Bryman, A. E. (2015). *Triangulation and measurement*. Department of Social Sciences, Loughborough University. Available from: http://www.referenceworld.com/sage/socialscience/triangulation.pdf.

Carmelli, D., & Page, W. F. (1996). Twenty-four year mortality in World War II US male veteran twins discordant for cigarette smoking. *International Journal of Epidemiology, 25*, 554–559.

Denissenko, M. F., Pao, A., Tang, M., & Pfeifer, G. P. (1996). Preferential formation of benzo[a] pyrene adducts at lung cancer mutational hotspots in P53. *Science, 274*, 430–432.

Egilman, D., Kim, J., & Biklen, M. (2003). Proving causation: The use and abuse of medical and scientific evidence inside the courtroom—An epidemiologist's critique of the judicial interpretation of the Daubert ruling. *Food and Drug Law Journal, 58*(2), 223–250.

Glymour, C., & Glymour, M. R. (2014). Commentary: Race and sex are causes. *Epidemiology, 25*, 488–490.

Gordis, L. (2013). *Epidemiology* (5th ed.). London, UK: Saunders.

Greenberg, R. S., Daniels, S. R., Flanders, W. D., Eley, J. W., & Boring, J. R. (2005). *Medical epidemiology* (4th ed.). London, UK: McGraw-Hill.

Greenland, S. (1999). Relation of probability of causation to relative risk and doubling dose: A methodologic error that has become a social problem. *American Journal of Public Health, 89* (8), 1166–1169.

Haack, S. (1998). *Manifesto of a Passionate Moderate.* Chicago, IL: Chicago University Press.

Hall, N. (2004). Two concepts of causation. In J. Collins, N. Hall, & L. A. Paul (Eds.), *Causation and counterfactuals.* Cambridge, MA: MIT Press.

Halpern, J. Y., & Pearl, J. (2005). Causes and explanations: A structural models approach, part 1: Causes. *British Journal of Philosophical Science, 56*, 843–887.

Hammond, E. C., & Horn, D. (1984). Landmark article March 15, 1958: Smoking and death rates– report on forty-four months of follow-up of 187,783 men. By E. Cuyler Hammond and Daniel Horn. *Journal of American Medical Association, 251*(21), 2840–2853.

Hernan, M. A. (2005). Invited commentary: Hypothetical interventions to define causal effects-afterthought or prerequisite? *American Journal of Epidemiology, 162*, 618–620.

Hernan, M. A., & Robins, J. M. (2015). *Causal inference.* http://cdn1.sph.harvard.edu/wp-content/uploads/sites/1268/2015/07/hernanrobins_v1.10.29.pdf. (July 1, 2016, date last accessed).

Hernan, M. A., & Taubman, S. L. (2008). Does obesity shorten life? The importance of well-defined interventions to answer causal questions. *International Journal of Obesity (Lond.), 32*(Suppl. 3), S8–S14.

Howe, L. D., Matijasevich, A., Tilling, K., et al. (2012). Maternal smoking during pregnancy and offspring trajectories of height and adiposity: Comparing maternal and paternal associations. *International Journal of Epidemiology, 41*, 722–732.

Hume, D. (1975). Enquiries concerning human understanding and concerning the principles of morals. In L. A. Selby-Bigge (Ed.), *An enquiry concerning the principles of morals* (3rd ed.). Oxford, UK: Oxford University Press.

Imbens, G. W., & Rubin, D. B. (2015). *Causal inference for statistics, social, and biomedical sciences: An introduction.* London, UK: Cambridge University Press.

Jasanoff, S. (1995). *Science at the bar: Law, science, and technology in America.* Cambridge, MA: Harvard University Press.

Kim, S. R. (2012). Admissibility of evidence and probative power of scientific evidence in the current law. *Journal of Criminal Law, 24*(4), 201–225. (In Korean).

Lee, I. Y. (2012). Brain images as legal evidence in criminal procedure. *Journal of Criminal Law, 24*(4), 255–277. (In Korean).

Lewis, D. (1973a). *Counterfactuals.* Cambridge, MA: Harvard University Press.

Lewis, D. (1973b). Causation. *Journal of Philosophy, 70*, 556–567.

Lewis, D. (2000). Causation and influence. *Journal of Philosophy, 97*, 182–197.

Lewis, D. (2001). *On the plurality of worlds.* Hoboken, NJ: Wiley.

Lilienfeld, A. M. (1957). Epidemiological methods and inferences in studies of non-infectious diseases. *Public Health Reports, 72*, 51–60.

Lipsitch, M., Tchetgen Tchetgen, E., & Cohen, T. (2010). Negative controls: A tool for detecting confounding and bias in observational studies. *Epidemiology, 21*, 383–388.

Lipton, P. (2004a). *Evidence to the best explanation* (2nd ed.). New York, NY: Routledge.

Lipton, P. (2004b). *Inference to the Best explanation* (2nd ed.). New York, NY: Routledge.

McAlister Gregg, N. (2001). Congenital cataract following German measles in the mother. 1942. *Reviews in Medical Virology, 11*(5), 277–283.

Morgan, S. L. (2013). *Eight myths about causality and structural equation models* (pp. 301–328). New York, NY: Springer.

Pearce, N. (1996). Traditional epidemiology, modern epidemiology, and public health. *American Journal of Public Health, 86*, 678–683.

Pearl, J. (2009). *Causality: Models, reasoning and inference* (2nd ed.). Cambridge, UK: Cambridge University Press.

Rothman, K. J. (1976). Causes. *American Journal of Epidemiology, 104*, 587–592.

Rothman, K. J. (2012). *Epidemiology: An introduction* (2nd ed.). Oxford, UK: Oxford University Press.

Rothman, K. J. (2014). Six persistent research misconceptions. *Journal of General Internal Medicine, 29,* 1060–1064.

Rothman, K. J., Greenland, S., & Lash, T. L. (Eds.). (2008). *Modern epidemiology* (3rd ed.). New York, NY: Lippincott Williams & Wilkins.

Schaffer, J. (2005). Contrastive causation. *Philosophical Review, 114,* 297–328.

Schneeweiss, S., Seeger, J. D., Landon, J., & Walker, A. M. (2008). Aprotinin during coronary-artery bypass grafting and risk of death. *New England Journal of Medicine, 358,* 771–783.

Spirtes, P., Glymour, C., & Scheines, R. (1993). *Causation, Prediction, and Search.* New York, NY: Springer.

Staessen, J. A., Wang, J. G., & Thijs, L. (2001). Cardiovascular protection and blood pressure reduction: A meta-analysis. *Lancet, 358,* 1305–1315.

Stamler, J., & Neaton, J. D. (2008). The Multiple Risk Factor Intervention Trial (MRFIT) – importance then and now. *Journal of American Medical Association, 300,* 1343–1345.

Stroup, D. F., Berlin, J. A., Morton, S. C., Olkin, I., Williamson, G. D., Rennie, D., et al. (2000). Meta-analysis of observational studies in epidemiology: A proposal for reporting. Meta-analysis Of Observational Studies in Epidemiology (MOOSE) group. *Journal of American Medical Association, 283*(15), 2008–2012.

Swygert, L. A., Maes, E. F., Sewell, L. E., Miller, L., Falk, H., & Kilbourne, E. M. (1990). Eosinophilia-myalgia syndrome. Results of national surveillance. *Journal of American Medical Association, 264*(13), 1698–1703.

Vandenbroucke, J. P. (2009). Commentary: 'Smoking and lung cancer'—The embryogenesis of modern epidemiology. *International Journal of Epidemiology, 38,* 1193–1196.

Vandenbroucke, J. P., & Pearce, N. (2015). POINT: Incident exposures, prevalent exposures, and causal inference: Limiting studies to persons who are followed from first exposure onwards may damage epidemiology. *American Journal of Epidemiology, 182,* 826–833.

VanderWeele, T. (2015). *Explanation in causal inference: Methods for mediation and interaction.* New York, NY: Oxford University Press.

VanderWeele, T. J., & Hernan, M. A. (2012). Causal effects and natural laws: Towards a conceptualization of causal counterfactuals for non-manipulable exposures, with application to the effects of race and sex. In C. Berzuini, A. Dawid, & L. Bernardinelli (Eds.), *Causality: Statistical perspective and applications* (pp. 101–113). Hoboken, NJ: Wiley.

VanderWeele, T. J., & Robinson, W. R. (2014). On the causal interpretation of race in regressions adjusting for confounding and mediating variables. *Epidemiology, 25,* 473–484.

Woodward, J. (2003). *Making things happen: A theory of causal explanation.* Oxford, UK: Oxford University Press.

Chapter 6
Epidemiological Causation and Legal Causation

Abstract In the fields of the philosophy of law and the philosophy of science, discussions of how epidemiological evidence related to causality is to be viewed by making use of counterfactual inferences have been underway since the mid-20th century. The strongest position regarding this, the potential outcome approach, argues that, with the exception of randomized controlled trials, causal relations must not be acknowledged when evaluating causality. On the other hand, the restricted potential outcome approach, adopting a more pragmatic stance, claims that when exposure to a particular factor decreases and the prevalence rate of a particular disease also decreases, that factor can be defined as one cause of the disease in question. However, both positions are limited in terms of how appropriately they can define interventions or clarify counterfactual hypotheses. Consequently, it is necessary to proceed to pragmatic pluralism for inferences to the best explanation. Here, models such as triangulation, negative controls, and the interlocking of evidence help to reach more comprehensive judgments on causal relations through epidemiological evidence.

6.1 Legal Proof on Causation with Epidemiological Results

Epidemiologists make estimations about causal relationships between risk factors and diseases. However, they only state that a particular factor can lead to a particular disease and do not speak of which factor has actually caused the plaintiff's disease. In lawsuits for damages, the causal relationship regarding the substance to which the plaintiff has been exposed and the disease from which he or she consequently has come to suffer, or a causal relationship, in the legal sense, is something that judges must determine. If so, then, can judges infer legal causation from epidemiological causal relationships? Once an epidemiological causal relationship between a harmful substance and a disease has been acknowledged, is the causal relationship between specific exposure to the harmful substance and the development of the disease on an individual level also considered to have been proven?

M. Jung, *An Investigation of the Causal Inference Between Epidemiology and Jurisprudence*, SpringerBriefs in Philosophy, https://doi.org/10.1007/978-981-10-7862-0_6

In Japan, in cases where an epidemiological causal relationship has been proven, legal causation is determined to exist between the harmful substance that has caused the disease in question and the development of the disease. For example, in a ruling that acknowledged a causal relationship between chromium VI (Cr6) contamination at workplaces and lung cancer among workers, the court stated that statistically significant figures had already been confirmed according to the results of epidemiological investigations and that Cr6 could be asserted conclusively as a carcinogenic substance according to animal experiments and genetic toxicity experiments as well. Therefore, it was ruled that there clearly existed a causal relationship between occupational exposure to Cr6 and liver cancer in the lawsuit.[1]

However, epidemiology is a discipline that studies populations and the correlations between particular factors and diseases, and epidemiological research results fundamentally consist of statistics on populations (Hall & Silbergeld, 1983). In general, it is inappropriate to make statistical inferences on individuals from research results concerning entire populations (Jurs, 2009; Greenland, Robins, & Pearl, 1999). For example, when the statistics that 70% of balls in an opaque box are red have been obtained from the results of sampling surveys, it cannot be said that the probability of the color of a ball taken out from the box and hidden in the hand being red amounts to 70%. The ball will be either blue or not. Even when the probability of the existence of a causal relationship between exposure to a particular risk factor and the development of the disease in the plaintiff is judged to be 50% based on an epidemiological study where the RR has been observed to be 2.0, the existence of a causal relationship in the legal sense cannot be stated based solely on this. Although it is commonly used in the natural sciences, probabilistic causal inference is an argument far removed from traditional legal principle regarding fact-finding. Major facts that courts acknowledge either exist or do not exist. This is because the possibility for the existence of a particular fact amounts to either 100 or 0%, not 30 or 70%.

It is still difficult for courts to make inferences about individual legal causation from epidemiological causal relationships. Nevertheless, it is excessive to claim that epidemiological research results cannot be used as evidence to prove legal causal relationships. Some believe that epidemiological research results can be used only as evidence to disprove the other party, not as evidence to prove requisite facts for the establishment of a liability for compensations (Jaffee, 1985). However, only the competence of evidence is called into question in civil lawsuits unless there are special circumstances, and this is dependent on judges' free evaluation of the evidence. Here, although judges must respect scientific facts or already proven probability, they do not necessarily have to exclude something just because it does not constitute generally approved scientific knowledge. This is because science and trials belong to fundamentally disparate time frames. Because science is a discipline that arrives at the scientific truth through hypotheses and verifications, given adequate time, the causal relationship between a particular harmful substance and the

---

[1]The Decision of the District Court of Tokyo 458 (1981. 9. 28.), p. 118.

development of a particular disease will become clear in terms of the natural sciences. Until that moment, the hypothesis regarding the existence of a causal relationship will maintain its status as a still unverified hypothesis. However, judges do not have the time to wait. In determining causal relationships as constituent elements of wrongful conduct, the South Korean Supreme Court has made legal value judgments on the level of who is responsible for compensations for damages that have actually occurred.[2] According to this legal principle, determining the competence of evidence of epidemiological research results in courts ultimately leads to the question of which elements are to be taken into consideration. Matters that must be taken into consideration to reduce errors and to determine the competence of evidence correctly in applying epidemiological research results in courts are as follow.

First, the study in question must be one conducted by authoritative epidemiologists using reliable methods (Dore, 1983). In addition, because the competence of evidence is higher for cohort studies than it is for case–control studies, judges must evaluate the results of appraisals by experts considering the differences in research methods.

Second, errors due to chance, biases, or confounders must be controlled appropriately (Federal Judicial Center, 2011). Even though epidemiologists strive to reduce them at the study design, data collection, and data analysis stages, errors inevitably occur. Judges must bear this in mind when examining the epidemiological figures submitted as evidence and determining their reliability.

Third, the RR derived from epidemiological research must reach a certain level. In American judicial precedents, legal causation has been seen as acknowledgeable only in cases where the RR is 2.0 or above or the attributable risk (AR) is 0.5 or above (Egilman, Kim, & Biklen, 2003; Black & Lilienfeld, 1984; Green, 1992).[3] On the other hand, in Japan, for "high probability," which is the degree of proof in the Code of Civil Procedure, the AR is seen as amounting to 80% or above. The AR can be converted into the RR. Because $AR = (RR - 1)/RR$, when the AR is 80%, the RR must be 5.0 or above. However, this confounds the probability of the existence of a causal relationship and the degree of the judge's conviction regarding the existence of a causal relationship, or the degree of proof. Of course, nor can it be stated with certainty that the existence of causal relationships in individual cases is negated just because the RR remains on or below a certain level. However, when epidemiological research results constitute the only evidence, the lower the degree of the association is, the more cautiously individual causal relationships must be acknowledged.

Fourth, the qualitative and quantitative homogeneity must be acknowledged between the risk factor to which the plaintiff allegedly has been exposed and the risk factor determined by epidemiological research results. The degree, duration,

---

[2]The Decision of the Supreme Court of Korea 81Da558 (1984. 6. 12.)

[3]Daubert v. Merrell Dow Pharm, Inc., 43 F.3d 1311 (9th Cir. 1995); General Electric Co. v. Joiner, 522 U.S. 136 (1997).

type (exposure at home or the workplaces), and method of exposure determined by epidemiological research must be identical to those claimed by the plaintiff (Dore, 1985).

Fifth, the plaintiff must be identical to members of the general population in terms of exposure to possible risk factors other than the one in question. For example, when people who have smoked half a packet of cigarettes a day for 20 years are selected as members of the exposed group for a study on the association between smoking and lung cancer, the research results cannot be applied to a plaintiff who has smoked one packet of cigarettes a day for 30 years. In general, when individuals who belong to the group studied differ from one another in the degree of exposure to risk factors besides the one in question, the RR obtained from the research results is only the average risk for that group and cannot be applied categorically to individuals belonging to it.

Sixth, the possibility of the development of the plaintiff's disease due to causes other than exposure to the factor in question must be excluded. If none of the research participants has a family history of cardiac disorders in a study on the association between smoking and cardiac disorders, the fact that genetic factors cannot cause lung cancer must be proven first in order to be able to apply those research results to a plaintiff with a family history of cardiac disorders.

6.2   Legal Proof on Causation Without Epidemiological Results

To prove causal relationships, scientific evidence including animal experiment or in vitro experimental results and case reports is submitted at times in addition to epidemiological research results. Although such data, too, can be used as evidence to prove causal relationships, their advantages and disadvantages must be understood adequately when determining their value as evidence (Green, 1992; Egilman et al., 2003).

Because animal studies are experimental studies instead of observational studies, the researcher can control the research environment and therefore reduce the possibility of biases that affect the results. In addition, dose–response relationships can be determined with certainty because the amounts of the risk factors to be administered to animals are adjustable. Another advantage is that the research time is reduced because animals have short life spans and reproduction is easy to accomplish with them.

In contrast, due to interspecific differences (i.e., sizes, life spans, metabolism), it is difficult to say for certain that the effects identical to those found in animal study results will occur in humans as well (Green, 1992). In addition, the presence or absence of a threshold effect, too, must be examined because the animals studied are exposed to the risk factor in question adequately to cause the disease in question in animal studies (Egilman et al., 2003). Consequently, in order to acknowledge the validity of animal study results, whether the animal selected is appropriate must be reviewed according to the harmful substance to be studied and its effect, and the animal's pathogenic resemblance to humans.

In vitro, experiments consist of laboratory tests of the biochemical effects of a particular factor on cells, bacteria, tissues, and embryos. An example is transplanting animal embryo cells, exposing them to a substance that causes deformities, and testing their effect on grafted tissues. Although inexpensive, these experiments are conducted in animals and therefore do not take into consideration the effects of the factor in question on pregnant human mothers and human placentae (Green, 1992).

Case reports can also help to establish causal relationships conclusively. This holds true when reports on the side effects of a particular drug are published in academic journals or recorded in the database of the South Korean Ministry of Food and Drug Safety (MFDS). However, case reports may originate from chance rather than reflect true causal relationships. Nevertheless, when the effect of a particular risk factor is strong, a causal relationship is established based on case reports alone.

6.3   Remarks

Epidemiological research results are imbued with social authority as are physicians' written appraisals, and statistics figures are seen as objective and highly reliable. However, even with epidemiological research results, the possibility of errors exists, and subjective interpretations can intervene in the selection of the groups studied, evaluation of the data collected, and interpretation of the results (Dreyer, 1994; Shafer, 1986). Consequently, epidemiologists at times disagree on the association between exposure to a particular risk factor and the development of a particular disease as well. At such times, the association is gradually determined through more follow-up studies. However, adequate consideration of the possibility of errors is necessary when epidemiological research results are used in lawsuit procedures as a ground for the argument for the existence of a causal relationship between the plaintiff's disease and a particular factor. In addition, there also are cases where epidemiological results only point at the statistical association between exposure to a particular risk factor and the risk of developing a particular disease without being able to determine the existence of true causality. Nevertheless, epidemiological research results are necessary for proving individual causal relationships, all the more so from the perspective of lawyering.

Epidemiology helps to establish rational and consistent standards regarding causal relationships by combining statistics with biological or medical knowledge and determining the causes of diseases that develop in humans. Consequently, epidemiology can have a certain role in proving legal causation if and when courts establish a set of standards concerning the problem of inferring legal causation from epidemiological causal relationships. Of course, epidemiology is still a discipline unfamiliar to most jurists, and courts have not yet engaged adequately in discussions on the appropriate role of epidemiology. Nevertheless, frequent are cases where, in lawsuits for damages due to harmful substances, there is no way to prove causal relationships except with epidemiological research results. Fact-finding is not dependent solely on probability. It comes about through experienced judges' intuition after a consideration of all other aspects including the nature of the issue at hand, the purpose of the system, and the nature of the judicial proceedings. Consequently, it is invalid to approach the legal principle of fact-finding probabilistically for establishing legal causation. It is necessary to understand epidemiological research results accurately in terms of their advantages and disadvantages and to evaluate their value as evidence wisely.

References

Black, B., & Lilienfeld, D. E. (1984). Epidemiologic proof in toxic tort litigation. *Fordham Law Review, 52*(5), 732–785.

Dore, M. (1983). A Commentary on the use of epidemiological evidence in demonstrating cause-in-fact. *Harvard Environmental Law Review, 7*, 429–448.

Dore, M. (1985). A proposed standard for evaluating the use of epidemiological evidence in toxic tort and other personal injury cases. *Howard Law Journal, 28*(3), 684–686.

Dreyer, N. A. (1994). An epidemiologic view of causation: how it differs from the legal. *Defense Counsel Journal, 61*(40), 43–44.

Egilman, D., Kim, J., & Biklen, M. (2003). Proving causation: the use and abuse of medical and scientific evidence inside the courtroom—an epidemiologist's critique of the judicial interpretation of the Daubert ruling. *Food and Drug Law Journal, 58*(2), 223–250.

Federal Judicial Center. (2011). *The reference manual on scientific evidence* (3rd ed.). DC: The National Academic Press. https://doi.org/10.17226/13163.

Green, M. D. (1992). Expert witnesses and sufficiency of evidence in toxic substances litigation: the legacy of agent orange and bendectin litigation. *Northwestern University Law Review, 86*(3), 643–699.

Greenland, S., Robins, J. M., & Pearl, J. (1999). Confounding and collapsibility in causal inference. *Statistical Science, 14*, 29–46.

Hall, K. L., & Silbergeld, E. K. (1983). Reappraising epidemiology: A response to Mr. Dore. *Harvard Environmental Law Review, 7*(2), 441–448.

Jaffee, L. R. (1985). Of probativity and probability: statistics, scientific evidence, and the calculus of chance. *University of Pittsburgh Law Review, 46*, 924–1082.

Jurs, A. W. (2009). Judicial analysis of complex & cutting-edge science in the Daubert era: epidemiologic risk assessment as a test case for reform strategies. *Connecticut Law Review, 42*(1), 49–100.

Shafer, G. (1986). The construction of probability arguments. *Boston University Law Review, 66*(3–4), 799–816.

Chapter 7
Conclusions

Abstract The development of the natural sciences has gradually shed light on previously unknown causal relations through scientific hypotheses and verifications. Consequently, given adequate time, the controversy over causal relations between harmful materials and diseases will be mainly resolved. However, judges cannot wait for this and must make legal value judgments on causal relations as a requirement for the establishment of illegal acts. In other words, the responsibility to compensate for damages that have actually occurred must be imputed to a particular party. According to what has been examined thus far, it is no longer possible to deny the competence of evidence by epidemiological research results in the risk society of today. In particular, the number of cases for which there is no way to prove causal relations except for epidemiological data will increase in lawsuits for damages due to harmful materials. Consequently, it is necessary to interpret correctly and to use rationally the results of epidemiological studies through an approach based on pragmatic pluralism, thus appropriately evaluating the evidential value of such results.

7.1 Concluding Remarks

The present study investigated issues including causality among tobacco companies' illegal acts, smoking, and lung cancer occurrence. In tobacco lawsuits so far, the burden of proof regarding negligence and a causal relationship has fallen on plaintiffs. Since the legislation of the Product Liability Act, however, the possibility for mitigating the plaintiffs' burden of proof has opened up. Nevertheless, this alone cannot prevent the immense socioeconomic cost incurred by smoking. It is necessary to enact a tobacco management law so that no-fault liability for compensation from tobacco companies can be acknowledged. In particular, it is fundamental that courts' accept methods of inferring causality based on the natural sciences and epidemiology in situations where a causal relationship cannot be proven easily. In particular, jurists must consider the application of population-based evidence presented by epidemiologists in lawsuits for redressing damages to

© The Author(s), under exclusive licence to Springer Nature Singapore Pte Ltd., part of Springer Nature 2018
M. Jung, *An Investigation of the Causal Inference Between Epidemiology and Jurisprudence*, SpringerBriefs in Philosophy, https://doi.org/10.1007/978-981-10-7862-0_7

individuals with diseases, thus bridging the gap between normative adjudication and scientific judgment in concluding a causal relationship. In addition, it is necessary to take supplementary measures through the social security system such as establishing the upper limits for liquidated damages in lawsuits and creating a relief fund for victims of smoking. Because epidemiological data are already used as courtroom evidence to a considerable degree in adjudicating occupational diseases (Bianchi et al., 1999), there is no reason not to do it in tobacco lawsuits as well.

This study examined the South Korean Supreme Court's recent judgment, which needs to be addressed mainly in three aspects. First, the South Korean Supreme Court gave the verdict that, because the evils of smoking constituted a fact already and publicly acknowledged throughout society, tobacco companies did not have a special duty of notice above citizens' awareness of the evils of tobacco. In a situation where the evils of tobacco have increased continuously in terms of public health, however, it is implausible that tobacco companies should be exempt from publicizing the ills of the product called tobacco themselves and from participating in such a social atmosphere. Second, the South Korean Supreme Court stated that because smoking was a non-specific disease, the plaintiff must prove the argument that smoking was the only cause of lung cancer. However, the Court's judgment in classifying diseases into specific diseases, due to particular causes, and non-specific diseases, due to multiple causes, seems to be far removed from the opinions of epidemiologists, who are the experts. If the probability of the emergence of lung cancer is very low for non-smokers but is very high for smokers, a causal relationship in disease emergence must be accepted even for non-specific diseases. The protection of victims can be considered more fairly when the causes of disease emergence are determined based on the results of studies conducted by mainstream epidemiologists instead of intuitive judgments on causal relationships according to the presence or absence of specificity. Third, the greatest problem that has emerged from the South Korean Supreme Court's recent sentence is an attitude that, while treating the levels of judging scientific and statistical causation and legal causation as separate, denies epidemiological evidence regarding the relationship between tobacco and lung cancer emergence in law courts. However, not all fields of jurisprudence disregard statistical evidence, and those including forensic medicine have a considerably wide scope in acknowledging such evidence. Considering these facts, the Supreme Court's recent judgment can be seen as the product of a lack of understanding of specifying causal relationships based on epidemiological evidence.

Diverse factors intervene in disease occurrence. In principle, no disease develops from a single cause. However, the fact that various causes intervene in disease occurrence does not reduce the causal influence of smoking on lung cancer. Smoking has a greater causal influence than does any other factor identified so far. In particular, this is even truer in the case of the three carcinomas currently debated in tobacco lawsuits: small-cell lung cancer, squamous cell lung cancer, and squamous cell laryngeal cancer. In epidemiology, Hill's considerations for causation have been used to determine causality (Porta et al., 2014). Consequently, when considerations such as biological plausibility, coherence with existing knowledge, experimental demonstration, and analogy have all been satisfied through diverse experiments, it is necessary to provide relief to victims suffering from diseases through the de facto inference of a causal relationship.

The magnitude of causal contribution of a specific risk factor with respect to disease occurrence is expressed in the form of the population attributable fraction. The present study examined ways of applying the population attributable fraction in data to individual levels. The population attributable fraction can be used to presume the probability of causation because there exists a certain relationship between the attributable fraction and the probability of causation (Rothman et al., 2008; Broadbent, 2013: 162–181). Consequently, when determining the causality of disease occurrence for individuals in court, it is necessary to acknowledge the admissibility of evidence held by the attributable fraction figures presented by epidemiologists. This is the way to meet public sentiments and to render society at large, which is healthier through the regulation of harmful substances.

The development of the natural sciences has gradually shed light on previously unknown causal relationships through scientific hypotheses and verifications. Consequently, given adequate time, the controversy over causal relationships between harmful materials and diseases will be mainly resolved. However, judges cannot wait for this and must determine legal value judgments on causal relationships as a requirement for the establishment of illegal acts. In other words, the responsibility to compensate for damages that have actually occurred must be imputed to a particular party. According to what has been examined thus far, it is no longer possible to deny the competence of evidence by epidemiological research results in the present risks of society. In particular, the number of cases for which there is no way to prove causal relationships except for epidemiological data will increase in lawsuits for damages due to harmful materials. As discussed above, there is considerable confusion in practical affairs regarding how epidemiological research results are to be analyzed and evaluated in proving causation. Especially, noticeable are the absence of methodology in analyzing and evaluating epidemiological research and the confusion in legal principles concerning the question of estimating causation in individual cases based on epidemiological research results. Consequently, it is necessary to interpret correctly and to use rationally the results of epidemiological studies through an approach based on pragmatic pluralism, thus appropriately evaluating the evidential value of such results.

7.2 Practical Implications

Today, many attempts are made to increase the use of science in the process of making judicial decisions. They consist, for example, of creating standards of valid scientific evidence, improving and expanding the selection of expert witnesses, and implementing education for judges. Because law pursues justice and science pursues the truth, respectively, the two fields are often contrasted dichotomously. While science is explanatory and stresses progress, law is regulatory and emphasizes procedures (Goldberg, 1987). In comparison with law, science is strongly open, systematically testing or verifying the objects of observations and accepting criticism and counterarguments regarding the conclusions derived (Schuck, 1993; Ayala & Black, 1993). As a result, there exists a gap between the two fields, and lawyers and scientists alike are discomfited by this situation. To overcome such a conflict, it is necessary to strengthen the standards for selectively discerning good science in law courts (Ayala & Black, 1993: 239; Schuck, 1993: 43–44).

In fact, in determining substantial truth, law and science are in a mutually constructive relationship. Both law and science have systematically developed procedures for finding evidence in their respective fields and deriving rational and persuasive conclusions from it. However, an important difference between the two lies in the ways in which facts are acknowledged or recognized. Unlike science, law must derive conclusions without fail within limited time. Consequently, the legal recognition process often ends with the conclusion that there is a lack of evidence or requests new trials (Ziman, 1968: 14–15). It is all too easy for what judges, who are legal fact-finders, can know to be limited to witnesses' statements in response to lawyers' questions. If witnesses state that black is white and countering evidence is not submitted, the evidence submitted to the law court states that black is white and the court must issue a verdict based on this evidence (Freeman, 1986: 123–124). Consequently, to win trials, plaintiffs must prove their arguments based on clear and convincing evidence. Though litigants who have the burden of proof to discern the legal liability must present evidence that is advantageous to them, at times, seemingly unreasonable verdicts can be made because of the value priorities of the legal system.

In highly advanced technological society, risk factors that are difficult to regulate constantly threaten citizens' health and safety. However, the regulation of lawsuits on such public risks is limited. This is because the legal system is more accustomed to punishing older, larger risks than to punishing newer, smaller risks (Huber, 1985). As with the American lawsuits concerning damages from dioxin, scientifically and technologically cased lawsuits cost much in expense and take much time for the verdicts to be issued (Gray, 1987: 1). In the so-called Daubert case law, where the US Supreme Court made a verdict in 1993, a new standard regarding expert testimonies' admissibility of evidence contributed considerably to the discernment of valid scientific evidence by judges.[1] In order to resolve points of contention in lawsuits, law courts must accept progress in science and technology along with social change. In the opinions of the public, lawsuits are reliable and valid means for solving social debates that ensue from the development of science and technology. Consequently, it is necessary to review developments in particular fields in science and technology in law courts with an open mind and, at times, to assume interpretational flexibility regarding them. Of course, what are important here are standards on valid scientific evidence.

---

[1] 61 U.S.L.W. 4805, 113 S.Ct. 2786 (1993).

Toxic torts have proceeded in the direction of gradually considering plaintiffs and making judicial evaluations agree with mainstream science (Foster et al., 1993; Sugarman, 1990). Indeed, in 1977, the Association of Trial Lawyers of America (ATLA) defined toxic substance tort litigations as constituting a special field in lawsuits (ATLA, 1997). If so, then what may be standards regarding valid scientific evidence? The first one is whether particular evidence leads to a generalized conclusion verified through large-scale samples. What is often pointed out in pathological studies is that these studies are conducted on a small number of subjects so that the admissibility of evidence is insufficient for verifying the actual correlation between exposure and disease. From scientists' perspective, this is a problem caused by low statistical power. Scientists therefore believe that it can be solved by conducting follow-up studies through large-scale samples or submitting stronger evidence to law courts through meta-analyses, which synthesize the results of diverse studies. The potential probability of exposure factors other than particular toxic substances to have caused disease can be reasonably restricted through randomized assignment or the adjustment of confounding factors. For example, in studies on the association between asbestos and lung cancer, epidemiologists derive scientific conclusions by regulating smoking behavior as a factor that can cause similar types of cancer. Consequently, law courts, too, must carefully make use of propositions that have become scientifically generalized through large-scale samples.

The second is whether general causation in scientific community is applicable to litigants' specific causation. The fact that toxic substance X causes disease Y is presented as statistical probability regarding the likelihood of disease onsets for those who have been exposed to the toxic substance in question. However, for this to have superior admissibility of evidence in law courts, it may become necessary to present corroborative evidence that exposure to the toxic substance in question has actually caused the disease in question. Exposure dosage and duration are important for proving particular causation, but these are often difficult to determine accurately. For example, when a farmer has been exposed to a toxic pesticide, it can be difficult accurately to grasp the exposure level or the degree (%) to which exposure to the substance in question, out of diverse substances, has contributed to the development of the disease in question. In addition, the degree to which the factor in question has contributed to the development of the disease in question can be presented through relative risk (RR) or attributable risk (AR). This can be used in law courts as concrete critical values such as RR = 2.0% and AR = 90%. Consequently, scientists' general causation can be applied to specific causation in lawsuits as well. When there is a consensus on critical values, as has been discussed above, lawsuits for damages from environmental pollution or chronic diseases can be used in not only class lawsuits but also individual lawsuits because of the particular nature of their causation. It may be a bias on lawyers' part to argue that inclusive causation is a necessary condition, not a sufficient condition, of individual causation (Kaye, 1992). The trend today is for scientific and legal positivists to broaden further the scope of application of general causation through statistical significance (Jasanoff, 1995: Chap. 6).

The third is whether scientific evidence is a rational means for the relief of victims in terms of legal policy. Amidst a trend of mitigating plaintiffs' burden of proof, the more scientific causation including epidemiology is acknowledged for its admissibility of evidence in law courts, the greater is the possibility of relieving victims. The legal system has responded to the progress of science and technology by applying legal principles developed through lawsuits between the two parties of plaintiffs and defendants in relation to new social risks. However, in order to relieve victims based on the ideas of justice and fairness, the transformation of legal principles in the legal sphere has become indispensable. For example, with respect to points of contention such as product liability, medical negligence, and environmental pollution, law courts have had to discern carefully conflicting arguments regarding causation and legal liability and to proclaim one party as the winner. Because of the influence of legal realists, the main function of tort litigations has come to focus more on compensation for victims than on the punishment of negligence since the mid-twentieth century. "Strict liability" has replaced carelessness, which is the main ground for compensating individuals who have received damages from defective products. "Product liability compensation" has become a means of effectively reducing threats to human life and health. By applying the standard of reasonable predictability, law courts have expanded the scope of liability for manufacturers when there are sufficient connections between plaintiffs and defendants.[2] It is often very difficult for plaintiffs to prove that they have received damages from particular defendants, and law courts have ruled that victims are eligible for compensation for profit gained by companies through harmful products (Jasanoff, 1995: Chap. 2). In the case of tobacco lawsuits, more liability was imposed on individuals in the past for smoking.[3] Today, however, the fact that smokers have failed to quit smoking due to the strong toxicity of tobacco is taken into consideration (see Appendix 1).

The development of science and technology has made it possible to elucidate the causation of disease on molecular and cellular levels, and the development of experiment equipments has made it possible to present physiologic evidence for the possibility of the development of disease even before the actual occurrence (Nelkin & Tancredi, 1989). However, there still are questions regarding whether lawsuits are appropriate methods for relieving victims exposed to toxic substances. While arguing that science must be dealt with more strictly, those who support the current tort litigation system want gradual change, to the extent that judges and lawyers will engage in mutual education and cultivate their technical capacity. However, radical reformers emphasize unscientificity in judicial judgments in such lawsuits and want the professional approach to be strengthened further. Either disregarding points of contention regarding causation generalized in the scientific community or holding preposterous skepticism regarding statistical evidence does not help to relieve

---

[2]Escola v. Coca-Cola Bottling Co., 24 Cal.2d 453, 462 (1944); Greenman v. Yuba Power Products, Inc., 59 Cal.2d 57 (1963).
[3]Summers v. Tice, 33 Cal.2d 80 (1948).

victims. Focusing on errors in scientific evaluations made in the tort litigation system, reformers argue that the only way to confirm the matter of responsibility in law courts is to delegate more decision-making to experts.

References

Association of Trial Lawyers of America. (1997). *Toxic Torts*. Washington, D.C.

Ayala, F. J., & Black, B. (1993). Science and the courts. *American Scientist, 81,* 230–239.

Bianchi, C., Brollo, A., Ramani, L., & Zuch, C. (1999). Asbestos exposure in lung carcinoma: A necropsy-based study of 414 cases. *American Journal of Industrial Medicine, 36*(3), 360–364.

Broadbent, A. (2013). *Philosophy of epidemiology (new directions in the philosophy of science)*. New York, NY: Palgrave Macmillan.

Foster, K. R., Berstein, D. E., & Huber, P. W. (1993). Science and the toxic tort. *Science, 261,* 1509–1510.

Freeman, R. A. (1986). *The eye of Osiris*. New York, NY: Carrol and Graf.

Goldberg, S. (1987). The reluctant embrace: Law and Science in America. *Georgetown Law Journal, 75,* 1345.

Gray, P. B. (1987, January 13). Endless trial. *Wall Street Journal*.

Huber, P. (1985). Safety and the second best: The hazards of public risk management in the courts. *Columbia Law Review, 85,* 277–337.

Jasanoff, S. (1995). *Science at the bar: Law, science, and technology in America*. Cambridge, MA: Harvard University Press.

Kaye, D. H. (1992). On standards and sociology. *Jurimetrics, 32,* 545.

Nelkin, D., & Tancredi, L. (1989). *Dangerous diagnostics*. New York, NY: Basic Books.

Porta, M. S., Greenland, S., Hernán, M., Santos Silva, I. D., Last, J. M., & International Epidemiological Association. (2014). *A dictionary of epidemiology* (6th ed.). Oxford, UK: Oxford University Press.

Rothman, K. J., Greenland, S., & Lash, T. L. (Eds.). (2008). *Modern epidemiology* (3rd ed.). New York, NY: Lippincott Williams & Wilkins.

Schuck, P. H. (1993). Multi-culturalism redux: Science, law, and politics. *Yale Law and Policy Review, 11,* 14–21.

Sugarman, S. D. (1990). The need to reform personal injury law leaving scientific disputes to scientists. *Science, 248,* 823–827.

Ziman, J. (1968). *Public Knowledge: An essay concerning the social dimension of science*. Cambridge, UK: Cambridge University Press.

Appendix

Review of the Tobacco Class Action Lawsuit in Quebec, Canada, and its Implications for South Korea

In 1998, smokers in Quebec brought a class action lawsuit that sought to establish liability on a collective basis against the tobacco industry in Canada. After a trial of almost three years, the Quebec Superior Court rendered a judgment in 2015 that changed history.[1] It is necessary to review the significance of this case, what the judge concluded, and what appear to be the key factors behind the smokers' success. The plaintiff's position was as follows: Tobacco is addictive, tobacco is deadly for 50% of its users, tobacco manufacturers lied about the health risks for 50 years and colluded to prevent effective public health measures, and tobacco manufacturers should be accountable for the choices they made which affected society. However, the position of the tobacco companies was as follows: Tobacco is a legal product, tobacco smoking is a free choice, everyone has known about the health risks since 1953, the companies did not cause people to smoke, and disease and conduct causation cannot be determined on a class-wide basis.

In fact, the plaintiffs charge the companies with a fault far graver than failing to inform the public of the risks and dangers of cigarettes. They allege that the companies conspired to disinform the public and government officials of those dangers, i.e., as stated in their notes, to prevent knowledge of the nature and extent of the danger inherent in cigarettes from being known and understood. The allegation appears to target both efforts to misinform and those to keep people confused and uninformed. During essentially all of the class period, the warnings were incomplete and insufficient to the knowledge of the companies. Worse still, they actively lobbied to keep them that way. This is a most serious fault, where the product in question is toxic, such as cigarettes. It also has a direct effect on the assessment of punitive damages.

---

[1]Cécilia Létourneau v. JTI-Macdonald Corp, Imperial Tobacco Canada Ltd., and Rothmans, Benson & Hedges Inc., Quebec Superior Court. Case No. 500-06-000070-983; Conseil québécois sur le tabac et la santé and Jean-Yves Blais v. JTI-Macdonald Corp, Imperial Tobacco Canada, and Rothmans, Benson & Hedges Inc. Quebec Superior Court. Case No. 500-06-000076-980.

© The Author(s), under exclusive licence to Springer Nature Singapore Pte Ltd., part of Springer Nature 2018
M. Jung, *An Investigation of the Causal Inference Between Epidemiology and Jurisprudence*, SpringerBriefs in Philosophy, https://doi.org/10.1007/978-981-10-7862-0

Tobacco companies argued that no proof has been found that tobacco smoking causes diseases in humans. This reflects the standard mantra of the industry at the time; the scientific controversy according to which the harmful effects of smoking on health were not exactly denied but, rather, were characterized as being complicated, multi-dimensional and, especially, inconclusive, requiring much further research. This slipped into the equation the idea that genetic predisposition and environmental factors, such as air pollution and occupational exposures, could be the actual causes of disease among smokers. The reaction of the Canadian tobacco industry was to continue its efforts not only to hide the truth from the public but, as well, to delay and water down to the maximum extent possible the measures that Canada wished to implement to warn consumers of the dangers of smoking.

Thus, it appears to be incontrovertible that, by adhering to the policy statement, these companies colluded among themselves on order to impede the public from learning of health-related information pertaining to smoking, collusion that continued for many decades thereafter. They thereby jointly participated in a wrongful act that resulted in an injury, which is a criterion for solidary liability under article 1480 of the Civil Code. In fact, even when the government began to admit that smoking had certain health risks in the late 1980s, it and the companies continued to sow doubt by insisting that science had never identified the physiological link between smoking and disease. Strong evidence existed at the time to support a causal link between cigarettes and disease, and it was irresponsible for the Canadian tobacco industry to attempt to disguise this Sword of Damocles. By working together to this end, the companies conspired to impede the public from learning of the inherent dangers of smoking and thereby committed a fault, a fault separate and apart from—and more serious than—that of failing to inform.

According to the article 19 liability of the World Health Organization Framework Convention on Tobacco Control, for the purpose of tobacco control, the parties shall consider taking legislative action or promoting their existing laws, where necessary, to deal with criminal and civil liability issues, including the provision of compensation where appropriate. Therefore, regarding tobacco-related damage and healthcare cost recovery efforts, in an action brought on a collective basis, proof of causation between alleged facts, in particular between the defendant's wrong or failure and the healthcare costs whose recovery is being sought, or between exposure to a tobacco product and the disease suffered by, or the general deterioration of health of, the recipients of that healthcare, may be established on the sole basis of statistical information or information derived from epidemiological, sociological, or any other relevant studies, including information derived from a sampling. This also applies to proof of the healthcare costs whose recovery is being sought in such an action. The Quebec Superior Court recognized that similar provisions in the British Columbia Act counteracted the systemic advantages under the traditional rules of civil liability that favor the manufacturers. These comments, although made in the context of common law, can easily be transposed to this case.

In conclusion, the assumption of risk by the victim, although it may be considered imprudent with regard to the circumstances, does not entail renunciation of his remedy against the person who caused the injury. Where an injury has been caused by several persons, liability is shared between them in proportion to the seriousness of the fault of each. Regarding aggregating damages, according to section 1031 of the Civil Code of Quebec, the court orders collective recovery if the evidence produced provides the establishment with sufficient accuracy of the total amount of the claims of the members; it then determines the amount owed by the debtor even if the identity of each of the members or the exact amount of their claims is not established. Therefore, where all members of the group have suffered the same type of prejudice, the prejudice can be assessed on the basis of an average without increasing the debtor's liability.

With the respect to the current status of tobacco litigation in South Korea, as of June 17, 2016, the last court date up to the present, the parties argued on the major legal issues during nine appearances, producing documentary evidence of the primary facts relevant to the issues. The two parties will argue the issue of the specific causal relationship between smoking and lung cancer based on the medical records of the insured produced by medical institutions before the court. The arguments will be followed by arguments of the issues of the tortious acts of the defendants during the subsequent court appearances.

Smoke from cigarettes was categorized as a Group 1 carcinogen by the International Agency for Research on Cancer. 71% of the chemical substances in cigarette smoke (approx. 2740 substances) are transferred through the thermal decomposition of tobacco leaves, and the remaining 29% (approx. 1135 substances) are transferred to smoke directly from the original substances. Cigarette smoke contains the following carcinogens: 11 Group 1 carcinogenic substances, nine Group 2 carcinogenic substances, and 48 suspected carcinogenic substances as categorized by the International Agency for Research on Cancer.

According to the WHO, *dependency* involves anxiousness and a desire for a certain substance and withdrawal syndrome and effects, thus including both physical and mental aspects. The fourth edition of the Diagnostic and Statistical Manual of Mental Disorders published by the American Psychiatric Association (APA) in 1994 finds that nicotine is a substance related to dependency and withdrawal effects but not involved with related symptoms such as acute poisoning, dementia or Alzheimer's disease, insomnia or anxiety disorders. Furthermore, in the tenth edition of the International Classification of Diseases issues by the WHO in 1992, *dependency on cigarette smoking syndrome* is categorized as a mental disorder. According to the literature, among smokers who successfully quit smoking, 90% did not require any help or assistance in quitting, and there were reports that the physical and mental dependency on nicotine is less than that associated with alcohol and that the physical dependency on nicotine is similar to that of caffeine. Dependency on nicotine was included as disorder or disease together with dependency on caffeine in 1994, and such dependency on nicotine was characterized as not involving physical dependency in the Report of the Surgeon General on Health published in 1964.

However, the Korean Supreme Court concluded that there exists no design defect in the manufacturing of cigarettes as regards product liability. The reasons for this finding were as follows. First, the original characteristic of cigarettes is the inhalation of smoke created by the burning of tobacco leaves. Second, the tastes of different types of cigarettes differ based on the amounts of nicotine and tar contained in each type of cigarette, and consumers smoke certain cigarettes based on their own flavor and taste preferences. Third, consumers smoke cigarettes with the intent to gain some medical effect of nicotine, such as a sense of stability that without nicotine they cannot enjoy. Fourth, even if nicotine and tar could be removed completely, tobacco companies' non-adoption of such a design cannot be deemed as a design defect. Fifth, there is no evidence to support that there exists a reasonable alternative design or that tobacco companies have failed to adopt such a reasonable alternative design which may have decreased the dangers or risks arising from cigarette smoking by consumers.

The Supreme Court also denied that there is a defect in the expression in cigarettes. The reasons were as follows. First, warning messages are present on cigarette packages, and these warning messages have become more intensified since 1976. Second, through the aforesaid reports and regulations, the fact that smoking cigarettes may cause diseases such as respiratory ailments, including lung cancer, was widely acknowledged by the general public. Third, cigarette smoking is a matter of the consumer's free will and choice despite the addictiveness of nicotine. Fourth, it appears that the fact that quitting smoking is difficult is widely understood and acknowledged by consumers.

According to the Supreme Court, cigarettes are considered as an item of personal preference in which not promulgating specific quality standards or limitations as to cigarette manufacturing has been permitted socially and legally, and such a legal system or the degree of social acceptance has not changed. It is difficult to find that cigarettes, an item of personal preference, lack ordinary stability or safety by reason of danger and harmfulness to health in that there are carcinogens in cigarettes and smoke or addiction which may arise due to cigarette smoking. Carcinogens can be found in unprocessed foods, and the amounts of carcinogens may increase upon the application of heat such that the existence of carcinogens in cigarettes cannot be deemed as peculiar. The traditional method of smoking tobacco using a pipe is similar to cigarette smoking, which involves the inhalation of smoke from burning tobacco leaves in which harmful substances have been created; such a method of smoking was not invented by tobacco companies. Even if nicotine dependency occurs, considering the seriousness of the dependency level or other symptoms or syndromes caused by the dependency, cigarette smoking can be deemed as an issue of personal preference and choice by one's own will.

In any event, if it is determined that there is a causal relationship between a certain risk factor and a certain disease, depending on the level of a higher incidence rate of such disease in a population exposed to such a risk factor as compared to an unexposed group—the possibility of such a risk factor being the cause of the disease can be inferred. However, the Supreme Court judged that *unusual (specific) diseases* are diseases that develop due to specific causes, and such specific causes correspond to the certain disease; hence, if it can be proved that a certain individual is exposed to the risk factor (cause) and the corresponding disease develops in the individual, a causal relationship can be inferred. However, *general diseases* are diseases that develop due to multiplicative causes such that even if the epidemio-logical causal relationship between the specific risk factor (cause) and a certain general disease is acknowledged, it cannot be inferred that the cause of the general disease is the specific risk factor (cause) as long as the possibility of exposure to other risk factors (causes) exists. In such an event, it must be proved that the certain general disease developed due to a specific risk factor (cause).

In conclusion, it is difficult to prove and proceed with arguments for common injuries or damage arising from a common cause in South Korea. In addition, there is no recognition of punitive damage and mass litigation (class action) for general tort liability (i.e., a limited or lack of remedies available for consumers against manufacturers' abusive acts). We find it difficult to investigate and prove liability due to the history of the government's monopoly on tobacco manufacturing and related businesses. These obstacles to current tobacco litigation in Korea must be discussed in greater depth.

Index

A

Abductive inference, 29
Acceptable risk, 27, 29
Adequate causation, 28, 33
Agent model, 10, 12
Air pollution, 3, 40, 58, 102
Attributable fraction, 50, 59, 60, 95
Attributable risk, 5, 42, 48, 50, 89, 97

B

Best explanation, 9, 16, 23, 78
Burden of proof, 2–4, 10, 35, 36, 38, 39, 57,
    58, 64, 83, 93, 96, 98

C

Carcinoma, 1, 4, 41, 79, 94
Case-control study, 49
Causal contribution, 59, 95
Causal inference, 6, 11, 64, 72–80, 83, 84, 88
Causal pathway, 9, 11, 23, 41
Causal pluralism, 83
Causal responsibility, 28
Clinical trial, 46
Cognitive subjectivity, 20, 22
Cohort study, 47, 52
Comparative negligence, 6, 58, 83
Component cause, 60
Confidence interval, 51
Confounding, 41, 51–53, 82, 97
Contrastivism, 77
Conventional relationship, 11
Counterfactuals, 73–76
Criminal negligence, 14, 28, 29, 31

D

Dangerousness, 14, 15, 29
Defoliant, 4, 40
Design defects, 56, 57, 61, 62

E

Empirical science, 15
Epidemiological evidence, 2, 4–6, 58, 64–66,
    72, 79, 81–83, 94
Event model, 10, 12
Explanatory function, 12, 33

F

Fact relevance, 29, 33
Factual causation, 10, 13–15, 29, 31–35, 39
Factual presumption theory, 3
Factual relations, 10, 12, 33
False omission, 28
Foreseeability, 13–15, 27
Framework Convention on Tobacco Control,
    63, 102

H

Hemophilia, 3, 40
Hill's criteria, 69, 72
Human understanding, 9, 23

I

Illegal act, 2, 10, 34, 35, 39, 61, 62, 93, 95
Impression, 18, 22
Imputation of responsibility, 10, 34
Increase in risk, 27, 29
Indirect fact, 37, 38
Induction, 15, 16
Inductive inference, 16
Information bias, 51, 52
Intended results, 13
Intentional offense, 31
Interlocking of evidence, 87
Intervening cause, 32
Intervention, 24–26, 31, 32, 37, 38, 46, 73–75,
    77, 78
Interventionism, 77, 83

L
Liability for default, 34
Liability of damage, 6

M
Manufacturing defects, 56
Medical malpractice, 10, 35–39, 57
Mind, 15, 17, 18, 20–22, 31, 72, 73, 89, 96
Mitigating demonstration, 37
Monocause, 59

N
Necessary conditions, 11, 60
Necessary connection, 17, 18
Non-fulfillment of contract, 35
Non-intervention, 38
Non-small cell lung cancer, 4
Non-specific disease, 4, 59, 62, 64, 94
Normative causation, 12, 13, 29, 31, 32
Normative relations, 12, 13, 33

O
Objective imputation, 10, 27–34
Observational association, 41, 51
Odds ratio, 48, 49, 70, 72
Overlapped causation, 28

P
Pictorial warning labels, 57
Potential outcomes, 72–74, 76
Pragmatic pluralism, 6, 73, 83, 95
Precluding wrongfulness, 15, 28
Premise circularity, 15
Prevalence rate, 46, 48
Priority, 9, 11, 17, 21–23
Probability theory, 3, 56
Probable relationship, 11, 12, 33
Product liability, 4, 40, 56, 57, 63, 66, 93, 98, 103
Propensity score, 79
Protective purpose of norms, 29, 30, 32
Proving of nonexistence, 5

P
Proximate causality, 14, 15
Proximate causal relations, 10, 30, 33, 34, 39
Proximate causation, 12, 14
Proximate cause, 2, 15, 24–26
Proximity, 9, 11, 17, 21–23, 33
P-value, 51

R
Redshift, 16
Regularity, 11, 20
Relative risk, 5, 6, 40, 42, 48, 50–52, 58, 64, 65, 70, 76, 97
Relief of right, 3, 5, 6
Relief of victim, 66, 98
Res ipsa loquitur, 3
Risk creation, 29, 30, 32
Risk realization, 28, 29, 32

S
Selection bias, 52
Self-defense, 28
Semantic theory, 21, 23
Significance level, 51
Sine qua non, 13, 14, 25, 28
Smoking-related lawsuit, 2
Specific disease, 4, 59, 62, 64, 66
Specificity, 4, 5, 60, 64, 71, 94
Statistical probability, 37–39, 97
Substantial cause, 13
Substantiality, 10, 14, 15, 29, 30, 32–35
Substantial probability, 36
Sufficient conditions, 11, 60, 74
Superiority of evidence, 3
Supreme Court, 3–6, 31, 32, 34, 36–40, 61–66, 80–82, 89, 94, 96, 103, 104

T
Temporal proximity, 37–39
Triangulation, 79, 80, 84

W
Warning defects, 56, 57, 62